When
FOOTBALL Was
FOOTBALL

STOKE CITY

First published in 2011

A catalogue record for this book is available from the British Library

ISBN: 978-0-857331-64-9

Published by Haynes Publishing, Sparkford, Yeovil,
Somerset BA22 7JJ, UK
Tel: 01963 442030 Fax: 01963 440001
Int. tel: +44 1963 442030 Int. fax: +44 1963 440001
E-mail: sales@haynes.co.uk
Website: www.haynes.co.uk

Haynes North America Inc., 861 Lawrence Drive,
Newbury Park, California 91320, USA

Images © Mirrorpix

Creative Director: Kevin Gardner
Designed for Haynes by BrainWave

Printed and bound in the US

When *FOOTBALL* Was *FOOTBALL*

STOKE CITY

A Nostalgic Look at a Century of the Club

Simon Lowe

Contents

Introduction by Terry Conroy

Looking back at old photographs is a wonderful way to both jog the memory and to introduce the younger generation into what it has meant to support Stoke City football club over the years.

Photos are evocative and enthralling split seconds behind which often sit great tales.

My favourite Stoke photograph features on page 136. It is of me dribbling around Hull City goalkeeper Ian McKechnie. We were 2-0 behind on a snowy day with the pitch a quagmire and half-time just seconds away. I was put through on the half-way line and ploughed through the mud to score – with no little poise and panache I'll have you know!

The goal completely changed the mindsets of both teams. At 2-0 up Hull were walking on air. Now we'd pulled one back you could see nerves already beginning to creep in as we walked to the dressing room for our half-time team talk.

We scored twice more in the second half through John Ritchie, who nodded in the winner from my cross, to win through to our first FA Cup semi-final in 72 years.

That picture encapsulates the moment, the spark of our great comeback.

What amazed me was how some very intimate moments were still captured for posterity all these years later. In this book I am pictured in my hotel bed, Alan Hudson is captured asleep on his settee and Gordon Banks is snapped receiving a huge bunch of flowers – from the opposing Chelsea team before our final against them at Wembley in 1972!

Pictures are the perfect way to capture such moments: Stan Matthews hanging up his boots aged 50, Neil Franklin returning from Bogota in disgrace, the horror of the Burnden Park disaster, Mark Stein's Wembley celebration and Mickey Thomas larking around in training are just a few highlights.

There is so much for young and old to discover in this book which stretches from the earliest beginnings in the 19th century up to the tearful farewell from the Victoria Ground in 1997. You won't be able to put it down!

Terry Conroy (jumping, stripes) and Jimmy Greenhoff tangle with Crystal Palace defenders John Sewell and Roger Hynd, watched by Stoke's Peter Dobing at the snow-covered Victoria Ground, the home of "the working man's ballet" in December 1969.

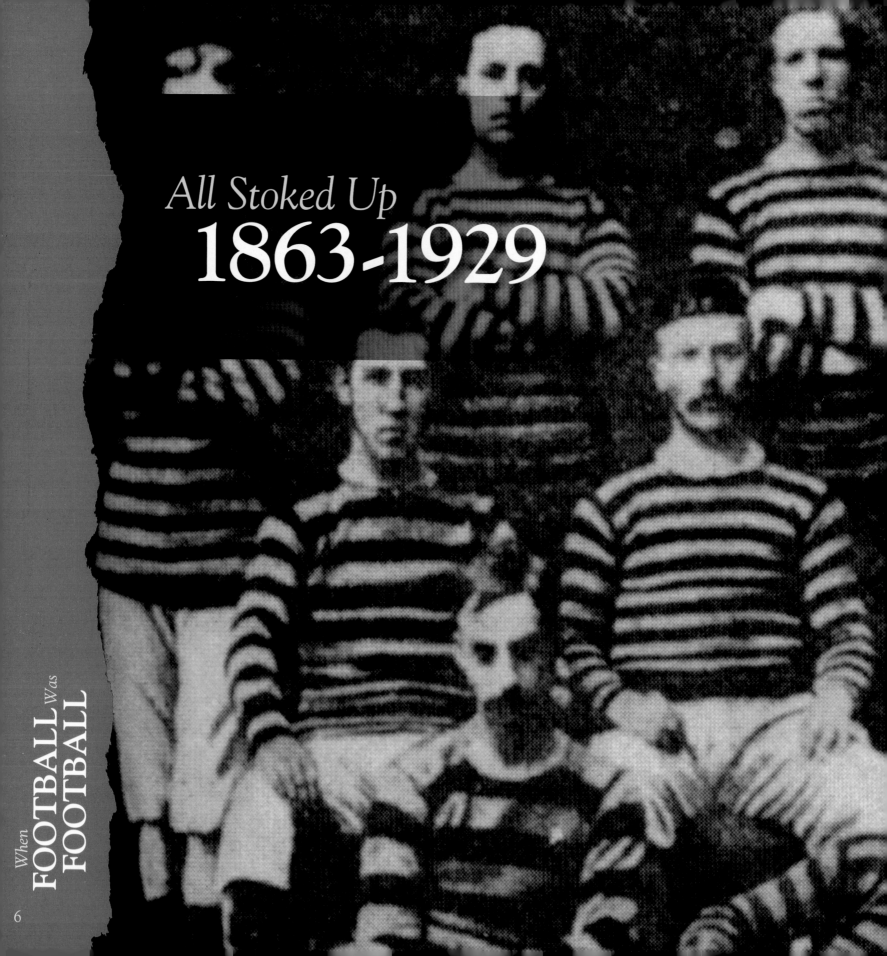

All Stoked Up
1863-1929

Stoke's first trophy winners: the 1878 Staffordshire Cup.

Captain Tom Slaney (seated on the left) was a schoolmaster at St Peter's School, Stoke, near the local church, and in 1874 took over as the prime mover in the Stoke club. Described as a "fine, dashing player", the tall, slender Slaney was also a "man of great geniality with a great sense of humour". On 28th March 1878, Stoke's first game at the Victoria Ground (until then the home of the Victoria Athletics club) was the first Staffordshire Cup final versus Talke Rangers. Stoke won 1-0. The winning goalscorer was William Boddington (seated centre, wearing a cap).

1863 The "Stoke club" founded. 1868 First recorded game. 1874 The dashing Tom Slaney becomes club captain and secretary. 1878 Stoke win the inaugural Staffordshire Cup in the first game to be played at the Victoria Ground. 1884 The club's first FA Cup tie. 1885 Stoke turn professional. 1888 One of 12 founder members of the Football League. 1889 Finish bottom of the first League competition. First England internationals. 1894 Strange transfer deal involving a set of wrought iron gates! 1896 Finish sixth in the First Division. 1897 "Gentleman Joe" Schofield becomes captain. 1899 Lose 1-3 to Derby at Molineux in FA Cup final semi-final after taking the lead. 1901 Playboy Dickie Roose joins Stoke. 1903 "Dirty Tom" Holford wins an England cap. 1907 Relegation from the First Division. 1908 The Stoke club folds due to lack of interest and reforms to play in the Southern League. 1914 Defeat Stourbridge 11-0 in an FA Cup preliminary-round match. 1919 Re-elected to the Second Division. 1922 Win promotion to the First Division. 1923 Player revolt over wages after relegation. 1925 Club renamed Stoke City after King George V grants city status to the six towns. 1926 Relegation from the Second Division. 1927 Win the Third Division (North) championship. 1928 Charlie Wilson scores 38 goals in a season to set a club record.

The "Stoke Club" Founded

1863 is the date the "Stoke club" is believed to have been founded by former pupils of Charterhouse School, which was then sited in central London, and who moved to the Potteries to become apprentices at the Stoke railway works. Full of vibrancy and enthusiasm as Victorians often were, the young men soon became involved with a football team called the "Ramblers", which was set up by the vicar of St Peter's Church, Stoke, one J W Thomas, who was also secretary of the local Victoria Athletic club. No formal records or reports survive, but this formation date – if true – makes Stoke the second oldest professional football club in the world, after Notts County.

17th October 1868

First mention in the *Staffordshire Sentinel* of "the Stoke club" or Stoke Ramblers, which noted that the "Stoke club" played versus Mr E W May's XV and drew 1-1; the first goalscorer to write his name into the annals of the club's history was Old Carthusian Henry John Almond, who was cited in *The Field* magazine as being one of the founder members of the club. This game lives on as Stoke's first recorded match. It was played at Sweeting's Field, on the outskirts of the town of Stoke. Stoke was the heartbeat of the Potteries, which had been made world famous by Josiah Wedgwood's Etruria factory, just up the canal.

The famous red-and-white stripes

Stoke first wore a deep red or maroon kit, but soon changed to red-and-white stripes, which were well established by the time the club joined the Football League. Strangely, in the 1891/92 season when clubs could only play in one kit, Stoke were forced to play in a black-and-amber striped shirt as Sunderland registered red-and-white first. The rules were changed after one season and home and away kits were introduced.

Into the Football League

After becoming one of the most prominent clubs in the country by playing friendlies and competing in the FA Cup, Stoke were one of the 12 founder members of the Football League. Club secretary Harry Lockett became the League secretary, and the first Football League offices were in Hanley. The club finished bottom of the first two championship tables and spent one year out of the League in 1890/91, returning after being voted back into the newly extended competition.

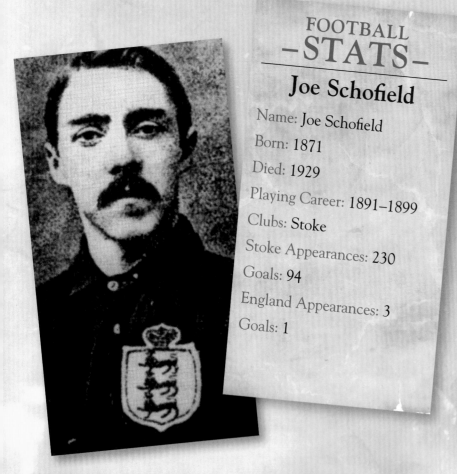

FOOTBALL
–STATS–
Joe Schofield

Name: Joe Schofield

Born: 1871

Died: 1929

Playing Career: 1891–1899

Clubs: Stoke

Stoke Appearances: 230

Goals: 94

England Appearances: 3

Goals: 1

Stoke's first England internationals were Billy Rowley (goalkeeper) and Tommy Clare (right-back), who played against Ireland in a 6-1 victory at Anfield on 2nd March 1889. Left-back Alf Underwood joined them – making what was regarded as the greatest defence at that time – to represent England against Ireland on 5th March 1892. This was the first time the back three had come from one club at international level.

–LEGENDS–

Joe Schofield

Winger and captain, later secretary-manager and director, Joe Schofield was a gentleman amongst Victorian footballers. A tricky outside-left, his play was cultured and clever, and he was known nationally as an entertainer with a bag full of tricks with which to confound and confuse opponents.

Schofield's classy play quickly brought him to the attention of the selectors and he made his England debut in March 1892 against Wales at Wrexham in a 2-0 win, the first of three caps. He scored one goal, against Wales in 1893, the last in a 6-0 rout. For three seasons to 1894/95, Schofield finished as Stoke's top scorer as the Potters established themselves as a mid-table team, finishing sixth in 1895/96.

His final tally of 84 League goals set a new club record, which stood for nearly 30 years. In 1908 he would become a director of the phoenix Stoke club.

The Stoke team, which played in the formative years of the Football League. Back row: (England internationals) Tommy Clare, Billy Rowley, Alf Underwood. Middle row: Charlie Baker, Davy Christie, Hughie Clifford, Davy Brodie, Billy Dunn. Front row: Lewis Ballham, Wilmot Turner, Alf Edge.

The Stoke reserve team "The Swifts" show off their silverware in 1892.

–LEGENDS–

Willie Maxwell

Scottish goalscorer Willie Maxwell arrived in a bizarre transfer deal with Darwen after Stoke agreed to buy a set of wrought iron gates for the hard-up Lancashire club's ground. Maxwell's upper-middle-class background gave him a liking for suits and a gentleman's stick, which earned him a reputation amongst the Stoke professionals as the quintessential dapper dresser.

His combination of physical presence and pace allowed him to develop into a fine individual forward in a Stoke side that struggled in the lower reaches of the First Division. His top-class goalscoring ability saw him notch double figures in five successive seasons from 1896/97, finishing as leading scorer on each occasion. In his best seasons of 1898/99 and 1900/01 he totalled 16 League goals, with three FA Cup goals, making his highest seasonal tally 19 in 1898/99. He eventually scored 85 goals for Stoke. Maxwell opened the scoring for the Potters in their first FA Cup semi-final in 1899, but Derby fought back to triumph 3-1 thanks to a hat-trick from Steve Bloomer.

Suspended for a fortnight for trading blows with a West Brom player and being sent off, Maxwell twisted his knee in a friendly game. He never fully recovered and was sold for £250 to Third Lanark to help ease the club's financial problems.

FOOTBALL –STATS–

Willie Maxwell

Name: Willie Maxwell

Born: 1876

Died: 1940

Playing Career: 1895–1908

Clubs: Clyde, Dundee, Hearts, Stoke, Third Lanark, Sunderland, Millwall, Bristol City

Stoke Appearances: 173

Goals: 95

Scotland Appearances: 1

Goals: 0

Stoke became known as football's "Houdini team" in the early years of the new century, after they continually avoided relegation from the top flight at the very last minute. Stoke finished just one place above the drop zone in 1901, 1902 and 1904, before finally succumbing in 1907. Pictured is the Stoke team of 1904/05, which finished in a relatively comfortable 12th position out of 18. From left to right: Frank Whitehouse, Tom Coxon, Fred Rouse, Teddy Holdcroft, Jack Whitley, Tom Holford, Arthur Hartshorne, Arthur Leonard, Jimmy Bradley, Harry Benson, George Baddeley.

FOOTBALL -STATS-

"Dirty Tom" Holford

Name: Tom Holford

Born: 1878

Died: 1964

Playing Career: 1898–1924

Clubs: Stoke, Manchester City, Port Vale

Stoke Appearances: 269

Goals: 33

England Appearances: 1

Goals: 0

–LEGENDS–

"Dirty Tom" Holford

One of the biggest stars of his era, Holford remains, at 5ft 4ins tall, the smallest man to play for England at centre-half. Tough, resilient and rugged best describe this defender for whom the over-used footballing moniker of "diminutive" is most apt. Tough-tackling Tom won his only cap on 14th February 1903 in a 4-0 win over Ireland at Molineux. During his 10 seasons at Stoke, Holford filled every position in the team, aside from goalkeeper, and his partnership with Jimmy Bradley and George Baddeley formed the basis for Stoke's survival in the First Division for eight seasons when the odds, due to the club's perilous financial situation, were that the team would be relegated. Holford was a popular figure with the Stoke crowd, setting a tradition of rugged, whole-hearted defenders. He was, remarkably, never sent off, although it should be remembered that the era was far more tolerant. Even so, Holford earned himself the nickname of "Dirty Tom". Holford became Stoke captain in 1904/05 and led by example. From March 1902 he missed just one game until March 1906. During that run he became the first player to play 100 consecutive League games for Stoke, achieving the feat on New Year's Day 1906. His run eventually totalled 105 games.

STOKE'S TEAM OF CUP-FIGHTERS

SPECIAL BY S. B. ASHWORTH.

It seems a remarkable thing that Stoke and Blackburn Rovers, still prominent representatives of the old school, have always missed each other in the national competition until this year, although it must be thirty years since they first met.

It was quite a Cup-tie, all dash and vigour, with skill for the time being thrown to the winds. The keepers had not much work, one reason being that the backs were very powerful safeguards. Another, the shooting was not "extra." The sides were very evenly weighted, and the ambition of either did not soar above a win by an odd goal. Sturgess shot this for Stoke from a twenty-yards range following a corner, and the lead was maintained, although Roose was called upon to perform a miracle shortly from the finish.

The forward play was not great, if Rouse is excepted, and this lion-hearted individualist was easily the pick. He is not afraid of having a try on his own. The halves were all good, Baddeley excelling, and Wolstenholme ran him very close. The Potters may cut a dash in the competition this time, for their side is built on the right lines.

13

–LEGENDS–

Dr Leigh Richmond Roose

The handsome and debonair "Dickie" Roose was one of the most famous amateur players of the pre-First World War era. The son of a Presbyterian minister, Roose won the first of his Welsh caps playing for Aberystwyth Town in 1900 whilst studying at university. There he earned a reputation as something of a ladies' man, openly flirting with the female students who flocked to watch him play. A self-styled exhibitionist, Roose dubbed himself "the entertainer" and, after moving to London to pursue a career as an assistant at Kings Hospital, he agreed to join First Division Stoke in October 1901. Roose's much-publicized arrival trebled the previous gate takings and the club's coffers began to fill again as word of the new star's antics spread – he took to sitting on top of the goalposts during injury breaks or throwing his boots into the spectators at the end of the game to entertain the crowds.

Roose was independently wealthy and so played football, in the true Corinthian spirit, simply for his love of the game. On one occasion, when playing for Aston Villa, he even hired his own train to get him to the game on time! Intent on a career in medicine he retired from League football at the age of 26 to concentrate on a three-year degree course at Kings, but was persuaded to return by Everton, who had a goalkeeping crisis when both their keepers were injured. He returned to play for Stoke after falling out with Everton's manager and won nine of his 24 Welsh caps during his two spells at the Victoria Ground.

Like many footballers, Roose was famously superstitious, wearing a "lucky shirt" beneath his goalkeeping jersey throughout the course of his career. The shirt, said to have been an old black-and-green Aberystwyth top, was reputedly never washed. He was far more sartorial in everyday life, often wearing a full Savile Row morning suit. In 1905 the *Daily Mail* named him as one of the capital's two most eligible batchelors alongside cricketer Jack Hobbs and Roose's relationship with music hall star Marie Lloyd – the Cheryl Cole of her day – sealed his reputation.

When war came, Roose served in the Royal Army Medical Corps and then joined the 9th Battalion of the Royal Fusiliers as a lance corporal. Roose won the Military Medal for action in France, but was killed in action on 5th October 1916 during the Battle of the Somme. His body was never recovered.

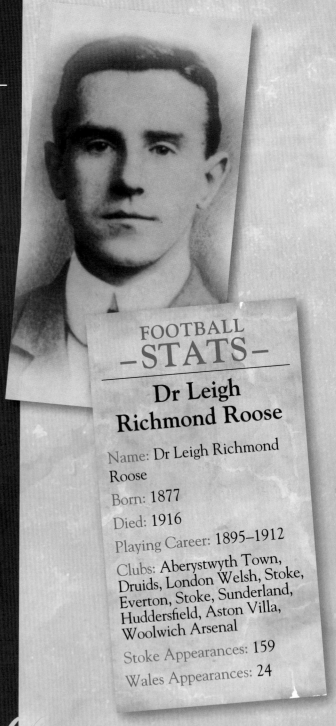

FOOTBALL –STATS–

Dr Leigh Richmond Roose

Name: Dr Leigh Richmond Roose

Born: 1877

Died: 1916

Playing Career: 1895–1912

Clubs: Aberystwyth Town, Druids, London Welsh, Stoke, Everton, Stoke, Sunderland, Huddersfield, Aston Villa, Woolwich Arsenal

Stoke Appearances: 159

Wales Appearances: 24

"
He really was a veritable Prince among goalkeepers.

Billy Meredith
"

Stoke's first playboy – Leigh Richmond Roose

A fishy tale

When Stoke visited Liverpool in January 1902 their goalkeeper's renowned medical skills were called into action when several Stoke players became violently ill after eating plaice for their pre-match lunch. Dr Leigh Richmond Roose, ailing himself, tended them, enabling the Potters to put a side out. It didn't help. Roose succumbed, with a pulse rate of 148, after just 10 minutes, with Stoke already a goal behind, haring from the pitch in search of a toilet. He didn't return and was replaced between the sticks by defender Sam Meredith. After half-time Stoke had just seven players fit to resume, although two later returned gallantly against doctor's orders. Stoke were hammered 0-7. "The dressing room resembled the cabin of a cross-channel steamer in bad weather … and smelt like it. Only more so," director Dr Moody told the press!

> "A good goalkeeper, like a poet, is born not made.
>
> Dr L R Roose

Ducked in the Trent!

On one famous occasion former Stoke amateur goalkeeper Leigh Richmond Roose's desire simply to play a game of football saw him fall foul of the burgeoning Potteries rivalry. Roose agreed to play for Port Vale along with four other amateurs in the championship decider of the North Staffs & District League in which Stoke's reserve side competed in April 1910. Vale swept to a 2-0 lead with Roose performing heroics in goal but the incensed Stoke crowd objected to these dubious tactics of "packing" the Vale team with "ringers". Over 100 supporters swept onto the pitch, picking up former hero Roose and carrying him towards the River Trent intent on ducking him. It took the arrival of the local constabulary to prise Roose from the clutches of the mob, saving him from a watery grave, and removing him to the safety of the boardroom. The Staffordshire FA declared the championship void after Vale refused to replay the game and Stoke had the Victoria Ground closed by the FA for the first two weeks of the 1910/11 season. A bewildered Roose claimed that he had been told the game was a friendly and certainly not a winner-takes-all championship game!

> "Before going to war say a prayer. Before going to sea say two prayers. Before marrying say three prayers. Before becoming a goalkeeper say four prayers.
>
> Dr Leigh Richmond Roose, bon viveur and Stoke goalkeeper

finally relegated from the First Division in 1907. They folded the following season at the end of a struggle
...s sold off as the directors uttered phrases publicly such as "We must cut our coat according to our cloth." A...
...*nel*, the club died due to "lethargy and indifference" after only 2,000 supporters turned up for the final hom...
...8 season. The Board decided enough was enough. The Stoke public no longer deserved to have a football c...
...t so poorly. Stoke's resignation was handed to the League.

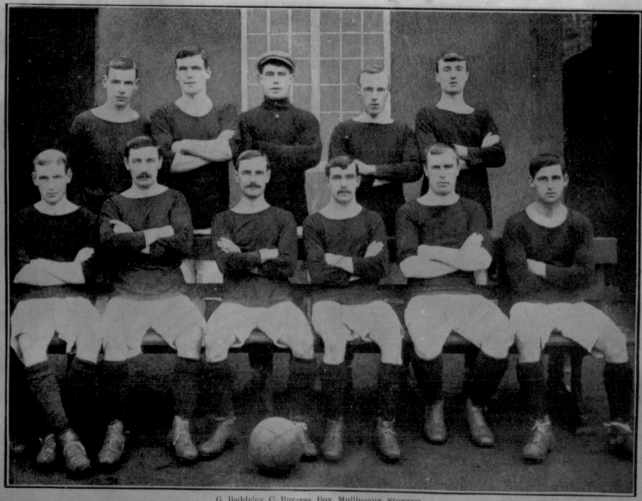

G. Baddeley, C. Burgess, Box, Mullineaux, Sturgess.
F. Fielding, Watkin, T. Holford, Chalmers, Gemmell, Griffiths.
STOKE.   Photographed by Scott and Co., Manchester.
Stoke were last in the First Division of the League last season.   Results of matches—8 won, 10 drawn, 20 lost.   Goals scored—For 41,
against 64.

The 1906/07 team which were finally relegated from the First Division after years of close shaves. Within a year apathy
had forced the folding of the club and its resignation from the Football League.

The Card

In the final scene of Potteries author Arnold Bennett's book *The Card*, published in 1911, hero Denry Machin helps to save a football club that is on the brink of going out of business. In the book the cheeky Machin makes his fortune by altering his school grades, stealing his employer's clients, inviting himself into Potteries society, setting up a newspaper to rival the existing one and arranging an accident for a car and claiming on the insurance. However, the scene in which he uses that wealth to rescue the ailing football club by bringing in the England centre-forward to great acclaim and hero worship is the most poignant as it mirrors the fortunes of Stoke FC in 1908. Stoke's demise left Stoke-on-Trent with no professional football team after Burslem Port Vale had gone under the previous year. Bennett may have been parodying the plight of the two Potteries clubs, but Stoke's real-life Denry Machin, the saviour of the club, was one Alfred Barker, who founded Stoke FC (1908) with the help of a number of other prominent men, including former captain Joe Schofield.

Stoke played in the Birmingham and District League and then the Southern League, with occasional appearances in the FA Cup, and often fielded two separate teams in different competitions. Their best victories were 11-0 over Merthyr Tydfil on 1st September 1909 in the Southern League and 11-0 over Stourbridge in the FA Cup preliminary round on 26th September 1914. The club played wartime football in the Lancashire Primary and Secondary competitions, which they won in 1918. Their best wartime victory was 16-0 over Blackburn Rovers on 10th November 1917. Seven Stoke players sadly perished during the First World War: Dick Herron, Henry Hargreaves, George Limer, Stan Ripley, Walter Nixon, Jack Shorthouse and Tom Kinson, plus Dr L R Roose, the former star. But participation in wartime football swelled club coffers to the point where new faces could be brought in and economic restraint was no longer the overriding factor. Stoke were re-elected to the newly expanded Football League when football resumed after the conflict in 1919.

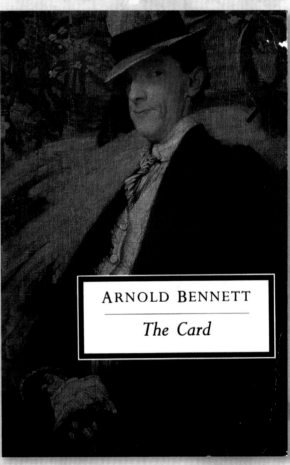

ARNOLD BENNETT

The Card

LEFT: Stoke in 1915/16. Note the mix of shirt styles indicating the austerity of the times.

FINISH OF THE LEAGUE FOOTBALL SEASON.

Stoke Go Up—Bristol and Bradford Relegated.

SAINTS FOR DIVISION II.

League football is finished—for fourteen weeks. The curtain was rung down yesterday in a blaze of sunshine, the kind of weather one usually associates with cricket.

Several things had to be decided yesterday, the chief being the second club to go into the First Division and the championship of the Southern Section, which carries with it a place in the Second Division.

Stoke won the right to accompany Nottingham Forest into the First Division by beating Bristol City 3—0 at Stoke.

At the same time they sent the City into the Third Division, for Coventry collected a valuable point at Selhurst against the Palace.

The football in the Stoke game was not good, but the Potters were the better side, and deserved their victory.

Thus, after appearing to be losing their chance of going up, Stoke recovered at the critical moment, and again become members of the League they helped to form in 1888.

In just the third season after the resumption of football Stoke won promotion back to the First Division. Stoke clinched second place behind Nottingham Forest by defeating Bristol City 3-0 in the final game of the season. Pictured left, Captain Tom Brittleton (in stripes) tosses up against South Shields before the 0-0 draw at the Victoria Ground on 22nd January 1921. Brittleton was one of Edwardian England's greatest players, having won silverware at Sheffield Wednesday, and he arrived at Stoke aged 38 and played for seven years, pioneering the long throw many years before Rory Delap. He was the driving force behind Stoke's promotion and "compelled respect" amongst the players. He eventually retired in 1925, aged 45, the then oldest player to appear for Stoke, only surpassed since by the extraordinary longevity of Stanley Matthews.

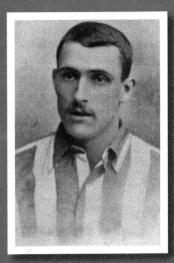

Tom Brittleton: Edwardian superstar and the second oldest man to appear for Stoke, aged 45.

The 1921/22 team, which won promotion. Back row: Tommy Broad, George Clarke, Bob McGrory, Gilbert Brookes, Alec Milne, J Beswick and a director. Front row: Dickie Smith, Fred Groves, Jimmy Broad, Arty Watkin, Billy Tempest.

-LEGENDS-

Jimmy Broad

Stoke were relegated from the First Division at the first attempt, despite centre-forward Jimmy Broad scoring 23 goals over the season, including one spell of 10 goals in five games. It was a cartilage injury picked up against Aston Villa in mid-February that put Broad out for the remainder of the season, which arguably cost Stoke their top-flight status. Compactly built at 5ft 8ins tall and 11st 12lbs, Broad appeared short to be a centre-forward. However, the game, at this time, revolved around inter-passing and running, skills that Broad possessed in abundance. He was the first player to score four goals in a League game for Stoke and he was also capable of the spectacular, once scoring from 35 yards out on the wing against Wolves. But he was also a character, leading a player revolt over wages following relegation and once missing a game because a bag of mothballs dissolved in his trouser pocket giving him nasty ammonia burns.

FOOTBALL -STATS-
Jimmy Broad

Name: Jimmy Broad

Born: 1891

Died: 1963

Playing Career: 1911–1929

Clubs: Stalybridge Celtic, Manchester City, Oldham Athletic, Millwall, Stoke, Everton, Barcelona, New Brighton, Watford

Stoke Appearances: 116

Goals: 67

-LEGENDS-

Arty Watkin

Arty Watkin played for Stoke for 12 years. A free-scoring forward, Watkin lashed in goals aplenty during Stoke's "wilderness years" outside the Football League, including five goals in the record 11-0 FA Cup victory over Stourbridge in 1914. He scored on his first appearance in the Football League, the decisive second goal in Stoke's 3-0 victory over Port Vale in the first ever League Potteries derby on 6th March 1920 and found the net twice in the crucial 3-0 victory over Bristol City that sealed Stoke's

FOOTBALL -STATS-
Arty Watkin

Name: Arty Watkin

Born: 1896

Died: 1972

Playing Career: 1913–1925

Clubs: Stoke

Stoke Appearances: 177

Goals: 77

promotion to the First Division in May 1922. But Watkin's patchy form and nervous disposition when one-on-one with opposing goalkeepers led to him being dubbed "an enigma". "The fact of the matter," wrote the *Sentinel*, "is that Watkin is the victim of a nervous temperament and it is only when the physical joy of the game obsesses him that he is seen in his best form. A goal from his foot has a magical effect and if it should be done early in the game he is just as likely to get a crop." Watkin was having problems coping with combining football and his work as a Pottery department manager at Grimwade's and once Stoke were relegated his employers put pressure on him to quit top-class football.

–LEGENDS–

Bob McGrory

Legend has it that when a dour, Scottish defender called Bob McGrory arrived in the Potteries, having been invited to consider signing for the club, he didn't like the look of the place from the second he got off the train at Stoke station after being subjected to the intense smog the bottle kilns occasionally spewed out. But he was persuaded to sign from Burnley by Stoke director Arthur Sherwin ... and didn't leave until 1952, after over 500 League and Cup appearances and 17 years as manager.

McGrory's influence bestrode four decades as captain for 13 seasons, coach under manager Tom Mather from 1930 until the latter's resignation in 1935, and then as the club's most successful manager to date. At the age of 41 he played in all 42 First Division matches in 1934/35, making him the oldest First Division player to complete a full season of games. McGrory made a club-record 511 appearances for Stoke, a record that stood for 24 years, but hung up his boots to take over the managerial reigns and created a team that came within one victory of lifting the League title in 1946/47. Indeed his team finished fourth twice, the highest-placed top-flight finishes of any Stoke side.

He was not without his peccadilloes, though. McGrory famously fell out with his star player Stanley Matthews, with both men's personalities grating on each other and McGrory jealous of Matthews' celebrity. The manager's decision to sell the most famous player in the world to Blackpool prior to the final, decisive match with Sheffield United in June 1947 arguably cost Stoke the chance of winning the championship, as a victory would have handed the Potters the title.

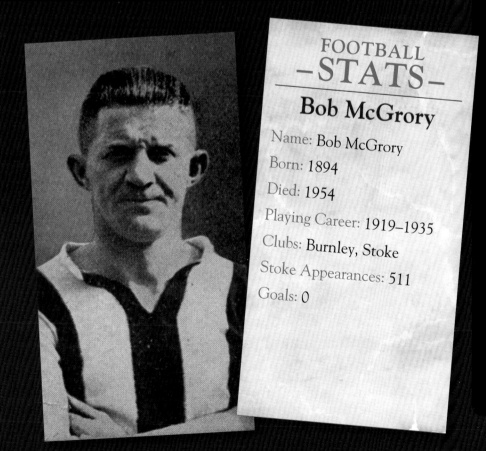

FOOTBALL
–STATS–
Bob McGrory

Name: Bob McGrory

Born: 1894

Died: 1954

Playing Career: 1919–1935

Clubs: Burnley, Stoke

Stoke Appearances: 511

Goals: 0

1925: Down to the Third Division

In 1925 the club added the suffix "City" to its name after King George V declared Stoke-on-Trent's six towns of Stoke, Burslem, Fenton, Hanley, Longton and Tunstall a city, but there was hardly time for celebrating this royal approval as Stoke were relegated to the Third Division (North) for the first time at the end of the season. Thankfully the championship and a quick return to the Second Division were sealed with a barnstorming campaign during which forward Charlie Wilson became the first Stoke player to score five goals in a League game in the 7-0 thrashing of Ashington on 25th September 1926. Stoke won 27 of their 42 games, scored 92 goals and finished with a record 63-point haul under the two-points-for-a-win system.

The squad that lifted the Third Division (North) championship in 1926/27. Back row (players only): Harry Sellars, Bob Robson, Foster, Bob Dixon, Peter Jackson, Reg Hodgkins, Len Armitage. Middle row: Dick Williams, Bob McGrory, Harry Davies, Charlie Wilson, Walter Bussey, Johnny Eyres, Cecil Eastwood. Front row: Tommy Dawson, Billy Spencer, Ernie Cull, Cliff Hallam, Harry Watson.

–LEGENDS– Charlie Wilson

In Stoke's first season back in the Second Division, Charlie Wilson netted 32 League goals and six in the Cup to total 38. This set a club record for the most goals scored in a season that still exists today. Wilson had arrived at Stoke from all-conquering Huddersfield Town, for whom he had executed 57 goals in 99 games. Wilson also top-scored in the following two seasons to become the first player ever to reach 100 goals for Stoke, reaching the landmark in a 1-3 defeat at Tottenham. He collected four more hat-tricks including a four-goal haul against Bristol City at Ashton Gate in February 1930. Wilson has the best goals per games ratio of any Stoke striker – 0.6 goals per match played. Perhaps his most famous moment came in February 1928 when Wilson sent "thousands of Stoke fans who had made the journey delirious with delight" when he fired home a spectacular goal four minutes from time to seal a memorable victory in an FA Cup fifth-round tie against Manchester City.

PLAYER'S CIGARETTES.

FOOTBALL –STATS–

Charlie Wilson

Name: Charlie Wilson

Born: 1897

Died: 1972

Playing Career: 1919–1933

Clubs: Coventry City, Tottenham Hotspur, Huddersfield Town, Stoke, Stafford Rangers

Stoke Appearances: 175

Goals: 121

PROMOTION FOR STOKE

Thompson Breaks Stockport's Net with Mighty Shot

Having spent a season in the Northern Section of the Third League, Stoke City yesterday qualified for promotion by defeating Accrington Stanley. Little was seen of Accrington in the first half, and Stoke's winning shot came just after the interval. Eyres then netting by kicking the ball out of the goalie's hands when he went down to save from Armitage. Powell sent in one for Accrington, but was ruled offside.

Rochdale were defeated at Walsall, and Bradford, by proving successful over Tranmere Rovers, take second place in the chart. Tranmere were narrowly beaten in a scrappy game, but spectators had value for their money, no fewer than eight goals being registered. McLean and Quantrill each obtained a couple for Bradford, and they won 5 3.

In the match at Chesterfield Thompson scored with such a mighty drive that it broke the Stockport net. Johnson also hit the Chesterfield bar with a terrific drive. Roseboom and Cookson also put on goals for Chesterfield, but Stockport failed to score.

Nelson have been threatening danger to many of their rivals for some time, but they came a cropper with Southport, and their chance went west.

Stan's the Man
1932-39

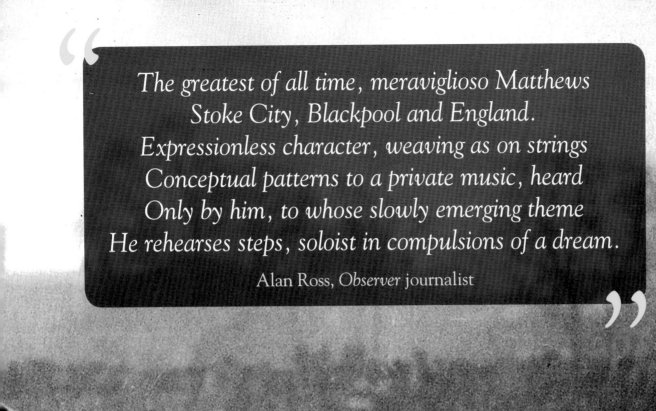

> The greatest of all time, meraviglioso Matthews
> Stoke City, Blackpool and England.
> Expressionless character, weaving as on strings
> Conceptual patterns to a private music, heard
> Only by him, to whose slowly emerging theme
> He rehearses steps, soloist in compulsions of a dream.
>
> Alan Ross, *Observer* journalist

1932 A 17-year-old called Stanley Matthews makes his debut away at Bury. **1933** Stoke win the Second Division championship. **1934** 84,569 watch Manchester City beat Stoke at Maine Road: the biggest football League crowd outside of Wembley. Stoke thrash bogey team Leeds United 8-1 in a League game. Goalscoring centre-forward Freddie "Nobby" Steele makes his debut for the club. **1935** Manager Tom Mather leaves to join Newcastle United. Bob McGrory is given the job of replacing him as player-manager. **1936** Stoke finish fourth in the First Division, a feat that has only been equalled once. **1937** Stoke thrash West Brom 10-3, the only time the club has hit double figures in the League. Freddie Steele sets a new club record, which has never been broken, by scoring 33 goals in a League season. **1938** Captain Arthur Turner misses his first Stoke match for three years after making 128 consecutive appearances: a new club record. Stan Matthews threatens to leave the club due to a dispute between himself and manager McGrory, leading to mass fan protests. **1939** Freddie Steele announces his retirement from football at the age of just 23, but is persuaded to return to Stoke after sessions with a psychiatrist. Stoke thrash Chelsea 6-1 on their way to finishing seventh in the First Division. War breaks out after Hitler's Nazi Germany invades Poland.

In 1938 Stan Matthews fell out with the club over the terms of his contract and asked to be placed on the transfer list. The prospect of losing the star winger prompted a mass meeting at the King's Hall with over 2,000 in attendance, led by a number of wealthy businessmen, who called upon the club to settle their differences and ensure the "Wizard of Dribble" remained a Potter. Eventually the differences were resolved and Stan stayed – for now.

The young Stan Matthews in the first known photograph of the footballing prodigy.

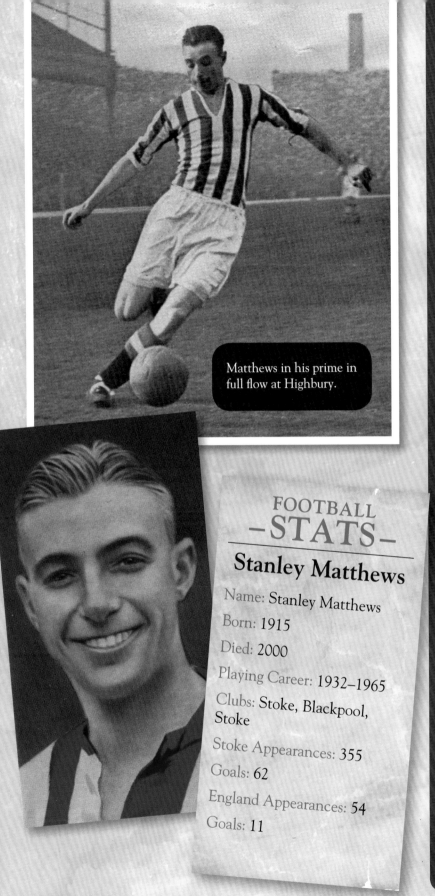

Matthews in his prime in full flow at Highbury.

FOOTBALL
-STATS-

Stanley Matthews

Name: Stanley Matthews

Born: 1915

Died: 2000

Playing Career: 1932–1965

Clubs: Stoke, Blackpool, Stoke

Stoke Appearances: 355

Goals: 62

England Appearances: 54

Goals: 11

-LEGENDS-

Stanley Matthews

Stanley Matthews is quite simply Stoke's greatest son. Famous worldwide for his incredible ability on the ball, Stan, as he was known to everyone, became a media darling and the first global symbol of everything that was good about football.

The 5ft 9in Matthews looked like a sleek greyhound with his hair, brylcreamed back onto his scalp, flaring up behind him as he exploded past his full-back. His skill was his supreme dribbling ability. It was as though the ball was tied to his feet with elastic. He would feint inside, drop his shoulder and race past his bamboozled opponent on the outside before whipping in a dangerous cross.

Matthews' astonishing ability brought numerous accolades from fellow players. Nat Lofthouse believed "the 'Wizard of Dribble' was the perfect nickname for Stanley. That's just what he was – a wizard who bamboozled defences with his ball control." Tom Finney agreed: "He could send an entire defence the wrong way with a shimmy, a sudden surge and clever dribbling. He laid on hundreds of goals." Danny Blanchflower expressed the frustration of facing Matthews: "You knew how he would beat you. You could not do anything about it, though."

Stan was quickly an England star, making his debut in September 1934 and going on to have an international career spanning 23 years, the longest for England. He scored a hat-trick against Czechoslovakia in a 5-4 win in November 1937, and was instrumental in England's 6-3 victory in Nazi Germany the following year. Now the world's most famous footballer, Matthews had become a cult personality. His image appeared everywhere and he made Stoke fashionable and famous across the globe. Even after his controversial departure to Blackpool, his name was synonymous with the Potteries – arguably one of his greatest feats was to make the smog and grim backstreets of Stoke-on-Trent seem glamorous.

Wilf Kirkham, Arthur Chadwick and Arthur Lewis, Stoke's newcomers in the summer of 1929; they formed the basis of the Stoke team that won promotion back to the First Division three seasons later.

Joe Mawson, centre-forward and top scorer in the promotion-winning season with 16 goals. He netted 50 times in his 93 appearances for Stoke overall before moving on to Nottingham Forest in September 1933.

In Stan's first full season, Stoke won promotion back to the First Division, defeating Lincoln 5-2 at the Victoria Ground on 22nd April 1933. Joe Mawson finished as top scorer with 16 goals, but when he was injured in February Stoke brought in Jack Palethorpe from Reading for £3,000 and the centre-forward netted eight goals in 10 games to propel City to the top of the division. Matthews scored his first goal for the club that season, at Port Vale in a 3-1 victory. Stoke returned to the top flight for the first time since being relegated in 1907, having suffered the ignominy of playing at places such as Ashington, Stourbridge, Pontypridd and Barrow-in-Furness in between.

Championship Winners!

The team that won the Second Division championship in 1932/33 included a young Stanley Matthews (middle row, second from right) and another star winger, left-sided Joe Johnson (back row, extreme left), who scored 15 goals that campaign.

Incredible Feats

The biggest crowd ever!

3rd March 1934: 84,569 watched Man City beat Stoke at Maine Road, the biggest crowd ever in England outside of Wembley Stadium. The occasion was an FA Cup quarter-final. The major attraction was wing sensation Stanley Matthews and his Stoke team. The only goal was scored direct from a corner by Eric Brook; goalkeeper Roy John blamed the blazing sun for him not keeping the ball out of the net.

–LEGENDS–

Harry Davies

Harry Davies became only the second man to score 100 goals for Stoke City, after Charlie Wilson, when he netted the second of his brace in a 3-1 win over Birmingham City at the Victoria Ground on 6th February 1936.

A quality inside-forward, Davies averaged a goal every four games for Stoke, where he quickly became a firm favourite. He had come to Stoke's attention while playing for Bamfords Athletic in the Uttoxeter Amateur League and made his debut in September 1923. He helped Stoke to win the Third Division (North) title in 1926/27 and his swashbuckling style attracted serial League champions Huddersfield Town, whom he joined in 1929. Davies scored 17 goals in 55 appearances in his three seasons at Leeds Road.

He returned to Stoke in early 1932, was instrumental in seeing the Potters win the Second Division in 1932/33 and remained a creative figure in Stoke's first team as the club established itself in the First Division. After losing his place to Jim Westland, Davies joined Potteries rivals Port Vale in February 1938. He retired in April 1939, after 49 games and five goals for Vale.

FOOTBALL –STATS–

Harry Davies

Name: Harry Davies

Born: 1904

Died: 1975

Playing Career: 1922–1939

Clubs: Stoke, Huddersfield Town, Stoke, Port Vale

Stoke Appearances: 410

Goals: 101

Stoke City.
med tränare och reserver.

H. Nuttall (Trainer).   Challinor.   Brigham.   Wilkinson.   Schrimshaw.   Mr. T. A. Preece (Director).   Soo.   Kirton.

The Stoke squad in 1937.

Back row (left to right): Hubert Nuttall (trainer), Jack Challinor, Harry Brigham, Norman Wilkinson, Charlie Scrimshaw, Mr T A Preece (director), Frank Soo, Jock Kirton. Middle row: Arthur Turner, Stan Matthews, George Antonio, Bob McGrory (manager), Freddie Steele, Jim Westland, Joe Johnson. Front row: Syd Peppitt, Billy Mould, Frank Baker, Arthur Tutin.

Thrashing Leeds

At the start of the 1934/35 season Stoke thrashed Leeds United 8-1 in their first home game, with the magical Matthews netting four times. He rounded three defenders and the goalkeeper to open the scoring, and then hit screamers from 25 and 18 yards before tapping in for the only four-goal haul of his career. In between he provided crosses for three of the other four goals as Stoke ran riot. The victory was especially sweet as Leeds were considered Stoke's bogey team at the time. Not surprisingly, given his outstanding performance, Matthews was selected for his first England cap the following month and scored as England defeated Wales 4-0 in Cardiff.

STOKE'S "HYMN OF 8"

Stoke City provided an early "shock" result by beating Leeds United 8—1 at Stoke last night.

Matthews, who opened brilliantly, scored two clever goals for Stoke in the first twenty minutes, the Leeds' defenders appealing vainly for offside when the second goal was scored.

Within half an hour Johnson and Sale had added further goals for Stoke against an unsteady Leeds defence Hornby, however, reduced the arrears before the interval, the ball rebounding from the post into the net.

Leeds played much better football in the second half, when the City defenders were often in difficulties, but Scattergood saved cleverly in the Stoke goal. Matthews and Johnson, however, missed easy chances for Stoke.

Sale added a fifth goal for Stoke from Matthews's centre and Matthews scored two more for Stoke before the end, and Johnson added the eighth goal.

Sale gave a great display in the Stoke team, and vied with Matthews for the distinction of being th... best player on the field.

Great Partnerships

The famous (from left) Arthur Turn, Arthur Tutin and Frank Soo half-back line.

Tutin, Turner and Soo

Stoke's rise from the Second Division to established First Division team was based upon what many believe to be the club's finest midfield in its history, made up of captain Arthur Turner, the diminutive Arthur Tutin and ball-playing Frank Soo.

Arthur Tutin was a pocket dynamo right-half. His tiny figure motored around the middle of the field picking up scraps of possession with which to feed his forwards. He was the least fêted of the famous Stoke half-back triumvirate, but he wielded considerable influence on Stoke's style of play in the heady days of the mid-to-late 1930s. A native north-easterner, Tutin, a stocky, powerful tackler, was no mere ball winner. He could also pass well and would support the attack alongside Soo, leaving the less nomadic Turner to hold the fort. His consistency almost matched Turner's. He missed only four games from the start of the 1934/35 season to March 1938. The war also cost Tutin arguably his best years and he retired in 1945.

Turner's massive 13st, 5ft 11in frame dominated the centre of every pitch that he entered. Stoke's "Mr Consistency" was not averse to using his physical attributes to his advantage and his rugged appearance put the frighteners on many opponents. Turner also prided himself on being the team's most consistent performer and he played 128 consecutive games for Stoke from April 1935 to March 1938 – a then club record, which has since been surpassed only once. He also took over penalty-taking duties from Tommy Sale and missed only twice, and on one of those occasions, against Everton in April 1936, he managed to knock home the rebound. He retired during the war after making 312 appearances and scoring 17 goals for Stoke, and went on to manage Oxford United into the Football League before joining Birmingham City.

Frank Soo was one of the finest left-halves in the country during his 12-year spell at the Victoria Ground. He was a strong and resilient player and a real crowd-pleaser. He was the first player of Chinese descent to appear in the Football League, but the outbreak of war curtailed his burgeoning career. Soo went on to play 81 wartime games, scoring 17 goals, and his performances earned Frank an England call-up, which eventually saw him capped eight times. But these appearances were never recognized as they did not take place during peacetime. Soo also played for the FA XI and the RAF and guested for a number of clubs, including Chelsea and Everton before, in September 1945, he signed for Leicester City for £4,600.

Stoke's other wing wizards: (from left) Joe Johnson, Frank Baker and Alec Ormston.

Wing Wizards

Although Stanley Matthews was the shining light of Stoke's great 1930s team, three other men won huge plaudits for their play over on the left wing: Joe Johnson, Frank Baker and Alec Ormston.

Joe Johnson began life as a fishmonger in his native Grimsby, playing for local side Cleethorpes Royal Saints. He quickly attracted attention and signed for Second Division Bristol City in the summer of 1929. Stoke acquired Johnson in the summer of 1932 and he became one of the final pieces of manager Tom Mather's promotion-winning jigsaw the following season. Johnson soon became known for his penetrating running style, which differed markedly from Matthews. Johnson would set off at full pelt, relying on speed to defeat full-backs. Like Matthews, however, he only had one really good foot, although in Johnson's case it was his left. Skilled and accurate, it also packed a rocket shot. Johnson won three England caps. He was sold to West Brom for £6,500 in November 1937 after picking up an ankle injury.

Frank Baker was an inside-left who earned his living driving a laundry van before Stoke manager Bob McGrory signed him. Baker's pace allowed him to take on his full-back and his crossing fed the voracious appetite of centre-forward Freddie Steele. He could score himself, too. In his first full season Baker bagged 11 goals and in 1938/39 he netted 10. After the war ended, McGrory moved Baker inside to replace Tommy Sale. Many observers considered Baker and Ormston to be the finest left-wing combination in England, and, in any other era, international caps would have been forthcoming. Neither, however, played for the national team, with Baker's inside-left position being staffed by an exceptionally gifted trio: Wilf Mannion of Middlesbrough, Chelsea's Roy Bentley and Sunderland's Len Shackleton. Latterly, Baker suffered from a run of ill luck with injuries, breaking bones five times in just over two years. He called it a day, aged 33, in the summer of 1951.

Baker's left-wing partner was Alec Ormston, whose peculiar crouching style, huddled over the ball with his body leaning forwards at a seemingly impossible angle, stemmed from his remarkable hunchback appearance. His opponents found little sympathy for the deformed 5ft 6in winger once he had sped past them. Ormston's major strength was his crossing; however, he could also tackle back, unusual for a winger in those days and entirely the opposite of Matthews. Ormston found himself called up to the Army in the summer of 1940 and made just a few wartime appearances for Stoke, although before he left Ormston cracked the winner in the vital championship decider against Manchester United when Stoke won the final game of the season 3-2 to clinch the Wartime Regional Western League by two points. In 1946/47, as Stoke challenged for the League title, Ormston scored 20 goals, including a hat-trick in a 5-2 win at Chelsea, making this by far his best season. In 1949/50 the chest illness that had begun in the forces restricted Ormston to irregular appearances and, aged 32, he moved on to Hereford in 1951.

–LEGENDS–

Freddie Steele

A prolific goalscorer, Freddie "Nobby" Steele holds the record for the highest total of goals scored for the club in the League, with 140, just three ahead of Frank Bowyer. A key driver of Stoke's successful 1930s team, he found the net 220 times in 346 matches overall, although many of these goals were scored in the war years, which he sadly lost to competitive football.

Manager Tom Mather spotted Steele's ability in the local leagues and in June 1933 the youngster signed professional terms. Steele made his debut against Huddersfield Town in December 1934, and it wasn't long before Freddie opened his goalscoring account in a Boxing Day victory over West Bromwich Albion. Once he started, Freddie didn't stop scoring. Steele set a new club record for League goals in a season of 33 in 1936/37, including four hat-tricks and a five-goal haul in the 10-3 mauling of West Brom. His performances soon won him a cap when, in October 1936, he made his England debut against Wales. In April 1937 Stanley Matthews and Joe Johnson were also selected to face Scotland – the first time since 1892 that three Stoke City players had been called up for England. Steele opened the scoring, but Scotland fought back to win 3-1 in front of a record Hampden Park crowd of 149,547. Steele would eventually win six caps, scoring eight times. His finest international moment came in a 4-0 victory over Sweden in Stockholm in May 1937 in which Freddie scored a first-half hat-trick.

Stan Matthews described Steele as one of the only footballers who could genuinely play with both feet, but not only could Steele score with his feet, he also racked up an impressive tally of headed goals. At 5ft 10in tall, Steele would spring into the air, tilt his head back and then whip the ball towards goal at a lightning speed. Many goalkeepers felt he could head the ball harder than some could kick it. He also boasted a tremendous turn of pace. His speed over a couple of yards was uncontested and took him away from struggling defenders.

Although he only managed to make 95 wartime appearances, due to his commitments to the army, Freddie came back stronger than ever for the transitional 1945/46 campaign, netting 49 goals in 43 appearances and then scoring a further 31 in 43 games the following season as Stoke almost won the League title. But a knee cartilage injury picked up in a challenge with Charlton Athletic goalkeeper Sam Bartram signalled the beginning of the end of Steele's career. In June 1949, Steele left the Victoria Ground and became player-manager of Mansfield Town before taking up a similar role at Port Vale. Steele proved himself to be an excellent manager, guiding Vale through their glory days when they won the Third Division (North) title and reached the FA Cup semi-final in 1954.

Striking Back

Incredibly, iconic centre-forward Freddie Steele announced his retirement from football due to depression in 1939. But a psychologist turned him around with therapy sessions and the rejuvenated England striker ran riot, scoring 10 goals in his first five games back.

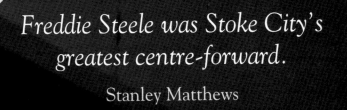

> "Freddie Steele was Stoke City's greatest centre-forward.
>
> Stanley Matthews

Powerhouse centre-forward Freddie Steele tangles with Arsenal defender Denis Compton at Highbury in 1938.

Goals, Goals, Goals!

The Stoke team of the 1930s were renowned for scoring goals, averaging 65 per season after their return to the First Division in 1933. There were some fantastic performances, including a 5-0 victory at Birmingham City in September 1935, a 6-2 defeat of Middlesbrough in September 1936 and an 8-1 thrashing of Derby in September 1937.

Tommy Sale was often on the scoresheet in these huge victories. Possessing a cannonball left-foot shot, Sale racked up 103 goals in 223 competitive appearances for Stoke in two spells at the club. He also added a further incredible 179 goals in 241 wartime games whilst working at the nearby Michelin car plant – an astonishing 55 goals came in 37 matches during the 1941/42 season, including one spell of four games in which he hammered home 14 goals (three hat-tricks and a five-goal haul). If you added his totals together then nobody has scored more goals whilst wearing a red-and-white shirt than Tommy Sale. However, wartime football was bereft of many top players due to their military service and so, sadly for Tommy, his wartime total cannot be considered alongside his peacetime one.

The man with the hardest shot in football, Tommy Sale (stripes), goes in where it hurts against Arsenal.

From left, Stan Matthews, Freddie Steele and Joe Johnson receive the congratulations of manager Bob McGrory after being selected to play for England against Scotland at Hampden Park in April 1937. Steele opened the scoring in the first half, but Scotland fought back to win 3-1 in front of a European record crowd of 149,547.

4th February 1937

Stoke hit double figures in the League for the only time in an incredible 10-3 victory over West Brom. The feat was completely unexpected as the side had been going through a lean spell and were also short of several players who had contracted flu. From the off Stoke ran riot and netted four goals before half-time before continuing to run riot in the second half. City were 10-2 up after 76 minutes, but took their foot off the gas after hitting double figures. There were some other notable firsts: Freddie Steele cracked in his first five-goal haul, most of them fed to him by Stan Matthews. George Antonio's brace were his first goals for the club and the inside-forward would also make his mark by scoring the only goal of the game when Stoke beat Arsenal for the first time in 1939. Joe Johnson, with two goals, and Arthur Turner, from the penalty spot, also found the net. As the 10th goal went in, the Victoria Ground erupted. After humiliating Baggies keeper Carey, the game became a changing-room joke for many weeks. Players would ask for the time and get the reply "ten past Carey"!

Two years later, Stoke were at it again when they thrashed Chelsea 6-1 at the Victoria Ground. Steele grabbed yet another hat-trick, one of a record 12 in Stoke colours, while Baker, Smith and Sale notched the other goals.

Stoke's team, which hammered Chelsea 6-1 in February 1939, with Freddie Steele scoring yet another hat-trick.

Trouble Brewing

Bob McGrory became Stoke's player-manager after Tom Mather left to join Newcastle United in 1935. In his first season in charge, McGrory propelled City to finish fourth, the club's highest ever finish, which has only been matched once since. But there was always an undercurrent of tension between the new boss and his star winger and eventually this boiled over into open warfare with Matthews refusing to sign a contract for the coming season.

In February 1938, there was a mass meeting of supporters at King's Hall to protest about what seemed to be Matthews' imminent departure. Surely Stoke couldn't be so short-sighted as to allow the best player in the world to leave?!

It appeared that the pair had fallen out because McGrory didn't like Matthews hogging the limelight, as he saw it, while the manager also had an axe to grind about Matthews having displaced his best friend Bobby Liddle from Stoke's line-up in the early 1930s. Eventually, though, the directors sorted out the situation and Stan declared he would stay, although the dislike simmered in the background.

STOKE CITY

Back Row (left to right)—Winstanley, Challinor, Westland (D.), Wilkinson, Scrimshaw, Kirton.
Middle Row—Matthews, Sale, Smith (C.), R. McGrory (manager), Westland (J.), Steele, Soo.
Front Row—Tutin, Ormston, Peppitt, Baker, Mould.

The 1938 Stoke team which was renowned for its panache and goalscoring ability.

The Stoke City golf day became a regular event during Bob McGrory's reign. But the manager (sixth from left) fell out with his star winger Matthews (eighth from right), leading to huge fan protests.

More Trouble Brewing

After years of posturing between German Chancellor Adolf Hitler and western countries, war finally broke out in Europe after Germany invaded Poland on 1ˢᵗ September 1939. Stoke's players were travelling back from Middlesbrough after drawing their third game of the 1939-40 season 2-2 at Ayresome Park when news broke; they were forced to endure a difficult journey without the use of headlights, which might have attracted the attention of German bombers, and arrived home exhausted in the small hours. The Football League was immediately suspended indefinitely and many of the club's players joined the forces, while Stoke itself helped the war effort by providing steel from the huge Shelton Bar production plant, manufacturing munitions at the nearby Swynnerton factory and taking in thousands of evacuee children from Manchester and Liverpool.

Designer Reginald Mitchell supervising work on his Supermarine Spitfire, just prior to his death in June 1937.

But the city of Stoke-on-Trent provided one other major contribution to the war effort – the designer of the Spitfire, Reginald Mitchell, was born in Kidsgrove, north of the city, and was educated at Hanley High School. The Spitfire was key to Britain's aerial superiority during the Battle of Britain as the German air force were fought off in 1940. It was a decisive victory, but the ensuing five years of war cost Stoke City dearly as the team that manager Bob McGrory had built, which finished seventh in 1939, lost out on its halcyon years, which could have brought in silverware by the bucketload.

RAF pilots scramble to take to the air to win the Battle of Britain in the summer of 1940.

The £10 Team

1940-50

> *My boys, my boys. They were wonderful days. They'll never leave me.*
>
> Full-back in the £10 team, Jock McCue

The £10 team: A squad made up of local players signed for just their £10 signing-on fee, which almost won the Football League championship in 1946/47.

1940 Stoke win the War League Lancashire section. Herod, Franklin, Mountford, McCue and Mould, members of McGrory's £10 team, make their debuts. 1941 Frank Mountford top scores with 23 goals in the season, does it again with 20 the following year and then converts to become a half-back to "avoid getting kicked"! 1942 Stoke defeat Everton 8-3. Tommy Sale scores 55 goals in 37 games and goes on to net 179 goals in 241 wartime appearances. Stoke lose 0-10 at Northampton. 1944 Freddie Steele scores 20 goals in just nine games. 1945 Neil Franklin and Frank Soo make their England debuts in a victory international against France, alongside Stanley Matthews. 1946 The Burnden Park Disaster sees 33 supporters killed when a crush barrier collapses during Bolton's FA Cup tie against Stoke. Matthews and McGrory fall out again, leading to the winger refusing to play for the club before relenting and returning to the fold. Franklin makes his full England debut against Northern Ireland. Stoke win 5-2 at Chelsea with Alec Ormston netting a hat-trick. 1947 The coldest winter on record forces the football season to continue on into the summer with Stoke in the hunt for the championship. Stanley Matthews leaves Stoke and signs for Blackpool for £11,500 just before the most important game in the club's history. Stoke come within one victory of lifting their first ever League title, but lose 1-2 at Sheffield United. 1948 The £10 team – Stoke field a side of players signed from local leagues, all of whom cost no more than their £10 signing-on fee. 1949 Frank Bowyer scores 19 goals in 22 games from midfield. 1950 Neil Franklin wins a record 27th consecutive cap for England.

McGrory's Local Lads Take Their Chance

Wartime saw the emergence at Stoke of a bevy of fantastic local players spotted by Bob McGrory's keen eye. Old heads such as Matthews, Steele, Johnson, Sale, Baker and Ormston were joined by the likes of Neil Franklin, Frank Mountford, Dennis Herod, Frank Bowyer, John McCue, Billy Mould and Johnny Sellars.

McGrory believed that if he could keep his youngsters together and give them valuable experience then, come the resumption of football in peacetime, his side would stand a far better chance of winning trophies. He was so nearly proved right.

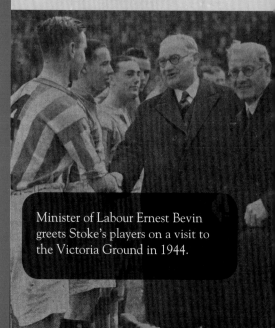

Minister of Labour Ernest Bevin greets Stoke's players on a visit to the Victoria Ground in 1944.

Left-back John "Jock" McCue was christened "Chopper" by his team-mates, two decades before Ron Harris of Chelsea earned the same nickname, as he crunched into tackles ferociously. During the war years he was an army PT instructor and fitness fanatic, combining his football with a job working for the British Coal Board, keeping miners fit. That fitness kept McCue as first-choice left-back until the grand old age of 35. If his 133 wartime appearances are added to his 542 official games for the club then John McCue played more matches for Stoke than any other player.

Baby-faced Billy Mould began life as a centre-half while Neil Franklin was serving His Majesty, but reverted to right-back after the war. Mould was renowned for his balance, powerful tackling and clearances. It was when he came into the side in 1946 that Stoke's defence gelled and a concerted effort was put in to reach the top of the First Division table. Mould picked up injuries later in his career and was released in 1952, aged 33.

Johnny Sellars followed in his father Harry's footsteps in playing for Stoke City. Born in April 1924, just four months after Harry signed for Stoke, Johnny grew up surrounded by the game. He joined Stoke in 1941 as a right-half, notching his first goal in March 1944 at Leicester. A natural athlete, the 6ft 2in Sellars had phenomenal strength, speed and stamina, which allowed him to cover every blade of grass on the pitch. Incredibly, given his voracious appetite for work, Sellars was only a part-time pro. He designed ladies shoes for the Lotus Shoe Company in Stone, 10 miles south of Stoke, while his pace and employment status allowed him to often compete in the famous Powderhall Sprint events, which featured sizeable cash prizes. Sellars played for Stoke until his career ended with a nasty eye injury received in the fifth-round FA Cup tie at Bolton in February 1958.

Given the Boot

A favourite wartime story revolved around a Stoke against Nottingham Forest match on 29th March 1941. Visiting manager Billy Walker, then aged 43 and having not played competitively for seven years, was forced to turn out for his team, who, despite borrowing three reserves from Stoke, were still one short. McGrory lent Walker his boots, which had remained in his office for six years since his own retirement. They didn't help Walker. Stoke won 4-0.

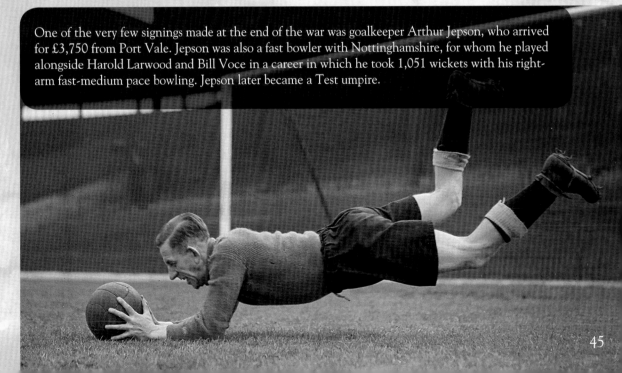

One of the very few signings made at the end of the war was goalkeeper Arthur Jepson, who arrived for £3,750 from Port Vale. Jepson was also a fast bowler with Nottinghamshire, for whom he played alongside Harold Larwood and Bill Voce in a career in which he took 1,051 wickets with his right-arm fast-medium pace bowling. Jepson later became a Test umpire.

Legendary centre-half Neil Franklin plays with his two-year-old son on waste ground near the Victoria Ground.

Brolly Wars

Whilst playing in a "B" international in Switzerland, Franklin almost started a riot after a withering tackle on the home winger Hiegenthaler. Responding to some theatricals from the Swiss player, a couple of beer bottles and an umbrella came flying down from the terraces in Franklin's general direction and a gathering mob looked likely to follow.

The situation was sorted when England keeper Frank Swift emerged from his goalmouth, armed himself with the brolly and warned the intruders to "Get back before I have to do something with this!"

–LEGENDS–

Neil Franklin

Arguably the biggest jewel in McGrory's crown at this time was Cornelius "Neil" Franklin, one of England's finest centre-halves ever. Perhaps only the more-fêted Bobby Moore rivals Franklin for his ability, poise and calmness when dealing with attackers.

Franklin was a radically different centre-half to those who had gone before him. In a time when almost every team in England possessed a raw-boned, battle-hardened centre-forward and clogger centre-half to combat them, Franklin was a gloriously refined exception.

For Neil Franklin was an outstanding footballer.

Much to Bob McGrory's frustration Franklin would only play one way, bringing the ball out of defence, using body swerves and feints more in keeping with wing play than with being a centre-half. It would often leave his manager spitting feathers on the touchline at the risks Franklin took.

But the crowds loved it. And mistakes were very rarely made.

Franklin stroked the ball around with masterful accuracy and viewed the hoofed clearance with disdain, except when strictly necessary. He believed the responsibility of "playing football" was as much his as the attackers in the side. Therefore, a dangerous centre into the Stoke penalty area was just as likely to lead to a counter-attack as a chance on goal.

During the war the young prodigy's star rose quickly and Franklin made his unofficial England debut in 1945 and won three wartime caps, but he cemented his place in the side during the victory internationals at the end of the war and became a permanent fixture in the national team thereafter. There were some great performances, both by Franklin and the team – notably in Portugal when England won 10-0. Franklin was also absolutely outstanding when England travelled to Italy and withstood a tremendous first-half onslaught before running out 4-0 winners in 1949.

Franklin was big buddies with Stoke goalkeeper Dennis Herod. Both were inveterate gamblers, although Herod would later tell tales of his poor luck and Franklin's Midas touch – something which also existed on and off the field until a decision in 1950, which changed the course of footballing history.

On 9th April 1950 Franklin set a record for successive England appearances at 27. He had never been left out by the selectors following his debut, at a time when players were dropped like confetti. Indeed, it is highly likely that Billy Wright was only able to attain his century of caps because Franklin decided to seek his fortune in Colombia, leading to him being ostracized by Stoke City and banned from playing for his country again.

FOOTBALL –STATS–

Neil Franklin

Name: Neil Franklin

Born: 1922

Died: 1996

Playing Career: 1936–1958

Clubs: Stoke, Independiente Santa Fe, Hull, Crewe, Stockport

Stoke Appearances: 142

Goals: 0

England Appearances: 27

Goals: 0

FOOTBALL
–STATS–

Frank Mountford

Name: Frank Mountford

Born: 1923

Died: 2006

Playing Career: 1940–1957

Clubs: Stoke

Stoke Appearances: 425

Goals: 24

Wartime Appearances: 183

Goals: 54

–LEGENDS–

Frank Mountford

Frank Mountford holds the unique distinction of being one of Stoke City's greatest centre-forwards, also one of the club's greatest half-backs and finally the trainer, under manager Tony Waddington, of the one team which won a major trophy in 1972.

After scoring on his debut in a 1-5 defeat at Tranmere, young striker Mountford went on to notch 53 goals during the war, top-scoring in 1940/41 with 23 goals and in 1942/43 with 20. This led manager Bob McGrory, not known for his public outbursts of praise, to call Frank another Freddie Steele. Mountford seemed set for a career as a prolific goal-scorer until he arrived at a momentous decision. He remembered: "I loved playing at centre-forward when I was younger, but when I played professionally and found out what it was all about I wanted to drop back and play in defence, where I could kick people rather than get kicked. My mother was all for it!"

Mountford's wholehearted, gritty style endeared him to his manager, although McGrory also used Mountford as a utility player, which meant that Mountford also appeared at right-wing, centre-half, inside-left, left-wing and left-half. Frank even played in goal for Stoke at Bolton after an injury to Dennis Herod.

Often seen flying through the mud to dispossess or flatten an opposing forward bearing down on goal, Mountford went on to become the club's trainer, much-loved by the stars of ensuing generations. His by-then silver hair would race across the turf as he tended injured players well into the late 1970s.

The Burnden Park Disaster: 9th March 1946

The bodies of the 33 dead are laid out on the Burnden Park pitch.

Bolton had won the first leg of this FA Cup quarter-final 2-0 at the Victoria Ground the previous Saturday and over 70,000 fans wanted to see the Trotters reach the semi-final on Saturday 9th March 1946. Because Burnden Park had closed the Burnden Stand, which ran along the length of the pitch, as it had been sequestered for use as a Ministry of Food store, fans had to cram tightly into the other three sides of the ground. Some areas were more popular than others and the Railway Embankment End was a natural focal point for Bolton fans flooding towards the ground. The terrace was little more than a shored-up mass of rubble and earth with occasional flagstone steps and, in places, wooden barriers in place of the steel girders that had perished to assist Britain's war effort.

With kick-off fast approaching, the embankment terrace almost full and thousands still outside, the clamour built to a frenzy as fans, desperate to get in to see the start of the game, began to take matters into their own hands. Hundreds threatened gatemen before climbing over the turnstiles, while the police pulled down many of those attempting to climb the fencing. Matters on the Railway

> "I knew those people hadn't fainted. I knew they were dead."
>
> Dennis Herod, Stoke City goalkeeper

The players leave the field as the tragedy unfolds.

Referee George Dutton, who took the players off the pitch and into the dressing rooms, but then told them to finish the game with bodies lying next to the pitch.

Embankment had become "pretty strained" soon after 2pm, with fainting cases occurring among men, women and boys who were passed bodily down, their sagging heads jerking perilously, towards the waiting ambulance men on the pitch. At around 2.45pm a 12-year-old boy, panicked by the developing crush, pleaded with his father to go home. The man, Norman Crook, picked the lock of the exit gates and left, but the opened doors allowed a torrent of fans to gain access to an already dangerously crowded enclosure.

At five to three, as the two teams emerged, the sudden incursion at the top of the embankment caused a surge forward and two of the wooden crash barriers collapsed under the weight of numbers. The crowd swayed like corn in the breeze before hundreds of spectators surged down the terraced steps towards the pitch. Spectators fell three or four on top of each other and were trodden underfoot as panic spread. A witness on the Railway Embankment itself recalled: "I was lifted off my feet and flung on the heads of those in front. I saw people on the ground and others sweeping over them, but nothing could be done to keep the crowd back. I could see men being crushed to death against the barriers before they gave way." "It was a horrible scene," blurted another witness. "Arms and legs were sticking out at odd angles and most of them were significantly motionless. I shall never forget the sight."

Ambulance men and police rushed to the aid of the crushed supporters. Stoke's goalkeeper Dennis Herod was guarding the net in front of the terrace where the incident had taken place and inquired of one policeman what was going on. "It's ok", he replied, "They've just fainted." But Herod knew the fate of the people now being laid behind his goal: "I'd served in North Africa, Italy and Normandy and I'd seen plenty of dead people. I knew those people hadn't fainted. I knew they were dead."

Play stopped and players stood around in groups watching as two police horses attempted to restore order and Bolton secretary-manager Walter Rowley appealed for calm. But as fast as the crowd receded at one point it eddied at another and more casualties dropped from the terracing onto the pitchside. The game clearly could not continue and referee George Dutton took the players off the pitch and to the safety of the dressing rooms at 12 minutes past three. Initial estimates from doctors put the death toll at 38, but it eventually reached 33 – more than had been killed in Bolton during the entire war – and left 520 injured in what was then the worst disaster English football had suffered.

The players eventually emerged to finish the game, but it was barely competitive, and Stan Matthews captured the poignancy of such deaths after the final whistle: "To survive a war, only to die at a football match sent a shiver running down the spine of nearly every one of us."

Stoke won 5-2 at Chelsea on 12th October 1946 with winger Alec Ormston netting a hat-trick and Steele and Kirton bagging the other two goals. The triumphant victory was notable because it announced Stoke as a serious title contender, but also because it was achieved without the injured Stan Matthews, giving manager McGrory the belief that the team did not necessarily need its star turn.

1947: Top of the League

Stoke's other right-winger, George Mountford (no relation to Frank), replaced Stan Matthews in the side when the England star was injured, but McGrory used the situation to force Matthews out, arguably costing Stoke the League title that season. As a right-winger Mountford was constantly compared to the genius of Matthews, but on the occasions when he filled in for the maestro, Mountford's completely contrasting style saw him run powerfully directly at opposing defenders, attempting to beat them for pace, rather than with ball trickery. He possessed a vicious shot and scored six goals in 23 games in the 1946/47 season.

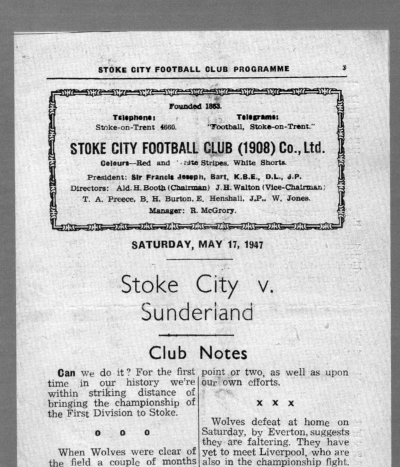

The programme for Stoke's final home game of the 1946/47 season. City could only draw 0-0, but Liverpool's win over Wolves meant that Stoke would lift the League championship if they won their last away game with Sheffield United.

The incredible 1946/47 season

In the first full League season after the war, 1946/47, Stoke's fantastic run of form propelled the club to the forefront of a four-way battle for the League title alongside Manchester United, Wolves and Liverpool. The season was notable because of the incredible twists and turns of the title race, the tumultuous weather – which ranged from deep and heavy snow to June monsoons – and the amazing flocks of crowds who came to watch football across the country. Over 40 million people saw League football that season. Stoke set a new club record with their highest-ever average League gate of over 30,000.

Controversy reined, however, in October 1946 after George Mountford replaced the injured Stan Matthews in the side at Chelsea and Stoke won 5-2 to announce their title credentials. Matthews then announced his fitness for the following game at Arsenal, but McGrory reignited the feud with his star winger by asking him to "prove his fitness in the reserves", via the press. Matthews was not best pleased and a stand-off developed, fuelled by rumour and counter-rumour, which dragged on and arguably affected Stoke's chances of lifting the title.

One of the last pictures of Stan Matthews playing for Stoke in the 1946/47 season, as he leaps over the close attentions of a Charlton defender in a 0-1 defeat in December 1946.

1947: Controversy as Stan Departs

Despite enjoying a fantastic season in 1946/47 it was evident that all was not rosy within the Stoke camp. Captain Neil Franklin was forced to scotch reports that some of Stoke's players thought Stan Matthews was sullen and too big for his boots, but eventually all the posturing came to a head and, astonishingly, Matthews was allowed to leave Stoke City.

He signed for Blackpool, where he had made his home after being posted there during the war, with the championship just one victory away. Even if Matthews had been openly detested – which he most certainly wasn't – it was simply bizarre to sell the best player on the planet with a League title within touching distance.

The fee of £11,500 was incredible for a player of 32 years of age, who was seen by some as nearing the end of his career, particularly as an attacking force. It was only just under the then record of £14,000, which Arsenal had paid to Wolves for winger Bryn Jones in 1937. McGrory clearly thought Matthews only had a couple of years left in the game. Just like the record producer who told the Beatles, 20 years later, that guitar groups were going out of fashion, this turned out to be one of the miscalculations of the century. Matthews had nearly 20 seasons left in him! A whole career for many.

Sports Mirror

Matthews: "All over"

THE Arsenal, in an eleventh-hour bid for the transfer of Stanley Matthews from Stoke City were told last night that no more offers could be entertained.

"Matthews has named Blackpool as the club to which he wants to go," said Stoke manager Bob McGrory.

"It is useless now for any other club to pursue the question."

Negotiations for the England winger's transfer to the Lancashire club are likely to be completed at a meeting today between the Stoke directors and Col. W. Parkinson, Blackpool chairman.

Matthews will be present. Discussion as to the fee which may beat the record £14,000 Arsenal paid for Bryn Jones will take most time.

LEFT: Stan Matthews is awarded the first ever Footballer of the Year trophy by Ivan Sharpe, president of the Football Writers' Association, but by the time he picked up the accolade the "Wizard of Dribble" was no longer a Stoke player, having fallen out with manager Bob McGrory and engineered a transfer to Blackpool.

BELOW: Matthews' England career was far from over. He earned his 54th and final cap in 1957 against Denmark in May 1957, aged 42 years and 102 days – a decade after Stoke let him leave. He remains England's oldest ever international.

1947: So Near, Yet So Far

Freddie Steele cracks a shot narrowly wide of goalkeeper George Swindin's goal during Stoke's 0-1 defeat at Highbury by Arsenal during the incredible 1946/47 season.

The Stoke squad that came so close to winning the League title in 1947, minus star turn Stan Matthews, who had been sold to Blackpool.

Stoke's season came down to one last game. Win at Sheffield United and the 1946/47 title was theirs. Anything less and Liverpool, whose campaign had finished a fortnight earlier would lift the title. But the Potters would have to win at the home of their bogey team – Sheffield United – without the talismanic Stan Matthews.

To that date, it was the biggest single game in the club's history, but it started badly when the Blades scored after only three minutes, goalkeeper Herod letting a tame shot slip past him. The custodian, who had survived a direct hit while on active service in the tank regiment in Normandy, blamed himself for years afterwards. Stoke, rampaging

Goalkeeper Norman Wilkinson, who had worked as a collier in his native Durham for most of the war and had barely been available to Stoke, had returned to the Victoria Ground after being demobbed on 26th October 1945 to find himself unwanted. Not only had he now reached the tender age of 35, but Wilkinson had lost over 2st in weight serving in France and had received a bad facial injury, which left him unable to open his mouth properly. As dental care was poor, and being in the wrong occupation to retain them for too long anyway, Wilkinson had lost most of his teeth. At first, or in fact second, glance he did not look like a professional athlete and Stoke now had three younger keepers on their books with first-team experience. The Board resolved to "get Wilkinson off our books at a reasonable figure". Wilkinson, however, was not prepared to go quietly and he took Stoke to court to enforce the law that those who had served would get their jobs back. Stoke had to acquiesce and Wilkinson was eventually re-engaged. There was dissention from two other veterans, too. Full-back Harry Brigham and forward Tommy Sale both asserted their right to re-engagement on full-time pre-war terms, although the Board minuted their thoughts that: "it would have been more patriotic if they had taken the part-time jobs found for them".

–LEGENDS–

Dennis Herod

At 5ft 9½in tall Dennis Herod was small for a goalkeeper, in fact one of the smallest Stoke has ever fielded. He made up for his lack of inches with acrobatic aerial saves and bravery that bordered on the nonsensical as his fearless plunging at the feet of oncoming forwards became a feature of his game. "I don't remember all the times I've been knocked out!" he often joked. On one occasion in March 1941 Herod rushed out to foil West Brom's forward W G Richardson. Badly injured, Herod took no further part in the game, and "The King", as his legion of fans on the terraces unsurprisingly dubbed him, spent a week in bed recovering from concussion, but then in his next game at Chester saved a penalty! He also turned one injury to his advantage when, in 1952, he was clattered by an opposing Aston Villa forward, broke his arm and was forced to play on the wing as there were no substitutes. With Villa pressing for an equalizer, Herod latched on to a long clearance, raced towards goal, beat keeper Con Martin and slotted home what proved to be the winning goal in a 3-2 victory.

forward through a raging gale and across a quagmire of a pitch, equalized through Alec Ormston before half-time. The Potters then laid siege to Sheffield's goal in an attempt to find the winning goal, but heartache followed when a long ball out of defence saw United's Walter Rickett one-on-one with Stoke full-back Jock McCue, who slipped over in a puddle, allowing the striker a clear run on goal. Rickett beat Herod to secure the win for the Blades and the championship for Liverpool. Stoke finished fourth in one of the tightest League title races ever.

Norman Wilkinson's contract, over which he took Stoke to court in order to get his job back after years serving in the army.

Final First Division table 1946/47

	Team	P	W	D	L	F	A	Pts
1.	Liverpool	42	25	7	10	84	52	57
2.	Manchester United	42	22	12	8	95	54	56
3.	Wolverhampton Wanderers	42	25	6	11	98	56	56
4.	Stoke City	42	24	7	11	90	53	55

The £10 Team

The famous incarnation of the £10 team was:

1. Dennis Herod (goalkeeper; from Tunstall)
2. Billy Mould (right-back; from Great Chell)
3. Jock McCue (left-back; from Stoke)
4. Frank Mountford (right-half; from Norton)
5. Neil Franklin (centre-half; from Stoke)
6. Johnny Sellars (left-half; from Stoke)
7. Johnny Malkin (right-wing; from Normacot)
8. Syd Peppitt (inside-right; from Stoke)
9. Freddie Steele (centre-forward; from Hanley)
10. Frank Baker (inside-left; from Stoke)
11. Alec Ormston (left-wing; from Hanley)

After Matthews' departure the magical spell that Stoke seemed to have was broken and the team never quite reached the heights of which it was clearly capable. However, one long-term achievement did arrive when McGrory was able to field a side made up entirely of players signed as apprentices by the club for just the £10 signing-on fee. This first occurred on 4th December 1948 against Blackpool. The local nature of the Stoke team was a matter of major pride in and around north Staffordshire – as it would be when the defence that lifted the League Cup in 1972 were all Potteries born and bred – and many have wondered why that kind of talent has disappeared from the region in the modern era.

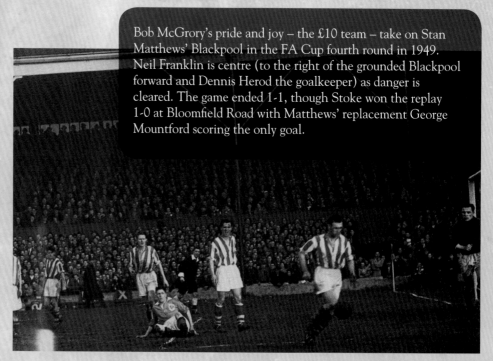

Bob McGrory's pride and joy – the £10 team – take on Stan Matthews' Blackpool in the FA Cup fourth round in 1949. Neil Franklin is centre (to the right of the grounded Blackpool forward and Dennis Herod the goalkeeper) as danger is cleared. The game ended 1-1, though Stoke won the replay 1-0 at Bloomfield Road with Matthews' replacement George Mountford scoring the only goal.

Six of Stoke's best young local players fill the Boothen End net: Standing: Johnny Malkin, Harry Meakin, Johnny Sellars, Roy Brown; Crouching Frank Bowyer and Frank Mountford.

Stoke's squad of players who only cost their £10 signing-on fee.

FOOTBALL -STATS-

Frank Bowyer

Name: Frank Bowyer

Born: 1922

Died: 1999

Playing Career: 1937–1960

Clubs: Stoke

Stoke Appearances: 436

Goals: 149

The Stoke Board shares the traditional loving cup ceremony, in which a drink is shared out of the specially made three-handled cup before the first home game of each new year, with Manchester City's directors. The tradition was begun by Stoke president Sir Francis Joseph (extreme right) in 1940 to "bring a little cheer in depressing times".

–LEGENDS–

Frank Bowyer

Although his career would last until the late 1950s, Frank Bowyer made his name when he burst onto the scene in the 1940s. An intelligent inside-forward blessed with a rasping shot in both feet, especially on the volley, Bowyer would go on to notch up the second most League goals for Stoke with 137, just three behind Freddie Steele and two ahead of John Ritchie.

In one golden spell from 8th September 1948 to 22nd January 1949, Bowyer scored 19 goals in 22 games. His volleying would often have supporters behind the goals at both the Boothen and Town Ends of the ground ducking as the net ballooned towards the terraces. Team-mate Frank Mountford remembered Bowyer as "a wonderful volleyer of a ball. His goals always seemed to be sweetly timed on the half-volley and I always thought personally that he was the best inside-forward I ever saw." Fellow youth team player, and later *Sentinel* sports editor, Peter Buxton, recalled another skill: "Frank could hit a long pass as accurately as any player in the game."

Remarkably ignored by England, Bowyer concentrated on scoring and creating goals for Stoke. But he missed out on the entire incredible 1946/47 season due to military service, which may have cost Stoke dear in the final analysis. Restored to Civvy Street in 1947, Bowyer top-scored the following season. He was a gentle man and kept pigs at his home in Newcastle-under-Lyme. In later years he dropped deeper and played a more creative role, although he top-scored in 1959/60 with 14 goals in his final season at the club.

Going to Pot
1950-60

An open goal goes begging as West Ham survive a close shave at the Victoria Ground in 1957.

> *I was that ashamed I didn't get the bus home –*
> *I walked.*
>
> Tony Allen, Stoke and England full-back, recalls yet another
> disaster in the 1950s

1950 Club captain Neil Franklin walks out on Stoke City and England to join the renegade Colombian League for a 500% salary increase but returns after the move goes disastrously wrong to be shunned by the football authorities and sacked by the club. 1952 Manager Bob McGrory retires and is replaced by Frank Taylor. Dennis Herod, injured and playing out of goal on the wing, scores the winning goal in a 3-2 victory over Aston Villa. 1953 Stoke are knocked out of the FA Cup by Third Division (North) Halifax Town. Stoke are relegated after Captain Ken Thomson misses a late penalty at home to Derby, which would have kept them up. Stoke sign forward Johnny King from Crewe and he goes on to score a century of goals for the club. 1955 Stoke win 6-0 at Bury in the Second Division, their biggest ever League away win. The never-ending Cup tie – Stoke finally beat 3-2 Bury in a fourth replay, after 962 minutes of play. Stoke win at Anfield for the first time in their history. Harry Oscroft scores 21 goals from the left wing during the season. 1957 Winger Neville "Tim" Coleman scores seven goals in Stoke's 8-0 thrashing of Lincoln City, the most goals ever scored in a match by a winger. 1958 Stoke knock FA Cup holders Aston Villa out at the third-round stage in a second replay. Dennis Wilshaw scores a hat-trick against Middlesbrough in the FA Cup and kicks Brian Clough up the backside! Stoke throw away promotion after topping the table at Christmas. 1959 19-year-old full-back Tony Allen wins three England caps. Stoke win 4-3 at Anfield, their second and last win at Liverpool's home ground. Legendary midfielder Frank Bowyer retires. 1960 After failing to win promotion for the seventh year in a row, Frank Taylor is sacked.

The Bogota Scandal

Internationally famous as the best centre-half on the planet, Neil Franklin, Stoke's captain, shocked the football world by controversially walking out on the club and joining Independiente Santa Fe in the renegade, unaffiliated Colombian League, for a reported king's ransom in salary in May 1950. The 500% wage increase both Franklin and team-mate George Mountford were reportedly to receive had been dreamt up by a Colombian diplomat named Luis Robledo – no relation to the famous Robledo brothers of Newcastle – who had attended Cambridge University and secretly married the daughter of a British aristocrat. Robledo had returned to Bogota an Arsenal and British football fan who believed that providing quality football could provide the answer to the continuing civil disobedience in Colombia – known as "*La Violencia*" – with British stars forming the main attraction. Franklin was offered £60 per week, plus a £2,000 signing-on fee, more than four times the maximum wage at home.

Although the money seemed too good to be true there were other considerations in Franklin's mind: "It wasn't really the money. I was unhappy at Stoke. The manager wanted me to change my style of play, but I reckoned if it was good enough for England then I should have been good enough for Stoke." As Colombia had been expelled from FIFA for poaching players from all over the world, the rebels found themselves suspended from playing anywhere within their jurisdiction. Franklin also felt the Potteries' air was not conducive to healthy living, as the local kilns continually belched out smoke and fumes, and he wanted to move his family away to a cleaner climate.

The situation was further aggravated when Franklin declined to join the squad for the 1950 World Cup finals in Brazil – England's first participation in the World Cup. The FA were not impressed.

Franklin was full of bravado on arriving in Colombia. "There's no future in Britain," he told waiting reporters, "We came because of the money and we are staying. We'll live finer than any footballers in the world." Despite a stupendous start, with Sante Fe winning 3-2 and the rebels leaving the pitch to shouts of "Long Live Britain", things did not work out in Colombia. The continuing severe political unrest and a 6.30pm curfew meant that the players could not socialize. There were problems with both the language and the diet: "It took us a couple of weeks to teach them how to cook bacon and eggs," recalled the recalcitrant Franklin. As the hoped-for El Dorado in Colombia proved to be a sorry illusion, in less than two months Franklin defected back to England, leaving behind an indignant Robledo who tempestuously resigned the chairmanship of Sante Fe "indignant at Franklin's contempt".

The reception back home wasn't much more welcoming. Chastened, largely ostracized and destined for virtual oblivion for the rest of his time as a player, Franklin would never play for England again as the FA were determined to make examples of the "Bogota Bandits". Stoke refused to let him return to the club, selling him to Second Division Hull City for a world-record fee for a defender of £22,500 in February 1951. Franklin was still only 29.

So what should have been one of the greatest, most recognized careers in English football descended into a sad, shambling mess. It should never be forgotten, however, that Franklin was a true great of English football.

Franklin and his family return to England after a terrible time in Colombia.

McGrory Retires

After a second consecutive successful struggle against relegation, long-serving player and now manager Bob McGrory retired in 1952.

McGrory's style of management was abrasive and contrasted starkly with his predecessor's. His tenacious personality ensured that Stoke's players never rested on their laurels, but also caused numerous disputes. He was also not afraid to give young players their chance. Early in his reign he replaced himself with long-term reserve full-back Charlie Scrimshaw, who had long been known as one of the best players outside the Football League. The emerging forward Freddie Steele edged out Tommy Sale at the age of just 19 and Frank Soo replaced the ageing Harry Sellars in midfield. It was brave management and it paid off as the young players gelled instantly.

Stoke were consistently in the top four, and, although they did not threaten to win the championship, they finished fourth with a new club record points total in the top flight of 47, and reached the fifth round of the FA Cup in 1936. In fact the defensive six of Wilkinson, Winstanley, Scrimshaw, Tutin, Turner and Soo played 30 consecutive matches together.

His team rebuilt through the spotting of local talent throughout the war years, McGrory led his men to within 90 minutes of the League title in 1946/47. His reign was undoubtedly the most successful in the club's history up to that point, but it is shadowed by his fall-out with his greatest star Stan Matthews, who threatened to leave in the late 1930s and then did depart in 1947 as Stoke were preparing to try to win the First Division championship for the first time in their history. McGrory had always believed in team over stars, but there was no doubt amongst his players, when asked after they had retired, that Matthews' sale had cost them the title as they fell just two points short. McGrory could still point to his two fourth-placed finishes being the only ones in the club's history. Could it have been better, though?

A taciturn Scot who was no stranger to dishing out the hairdryer treatment, McGrory died of a heart attack just two years later, aged only 59.

Part of the Potteries

ABOVE: Pots drying ready for decoration at the Minton pottery in Stoke-on-Trent. The trade, which gave the area its name, was still going strong in the post-war years and the football club kicked off home matches at 3.15pm so that potters leaving their shift could make kick-off.

ABOVE: Miners return to the surface after another gruelling day at the coalface of Hem Heath colliery. Ironically this would become the site for the construction of the new Britannia Stadium in the 1990s.

RIGHT: A typical Potteries backstreet in the 1950s. In this case children play in Loftus Street, Hanley. Players lived among the supporters and were "one of us", often travelling to the ground on the same bus as cars were out of the question on the £12 maximum wage footballers earned at this time.

Cup Humiliation and Relegation

Stoke have not been strangers to Cup humiliations over the years, but few rank alongside the 0-1 loss at Third Division (North) Halifax Town in January 1953. Stoke progressed easily enough into the fourth round of the FA Cup in that winter, defeating Wrexham, and must have thought their luck was in when they were drawn against Halifax Town, albeit away from home.

Things started going wrong the weekend before the Cup tie when regular keeper Dennis Herod picked up a bad leg injury in a 5-1 victory over West Brom in the League. That meant 23-year-old reserve goalkeeper Frank Elliott made his debut in goal at Halifax. Elliott had only signed professional terms with Stoke the previous Tuesday as he actually ran an ice-cream business, and had only played part-time since being released as a youngster by Swansea.

Elliott suffered the ignominy of conceding Priestley's goal at 42 minutes as Stoke lumbered to one of their most embarrassing FA Cup exits ever. To make matters worse over 8,000 Stoke supporters had travelled to the Shay to witness what they believed to be an almost certain victory.

The dreadful defeat also halted Stoke's League progress and City won just five of their last 15 matches, putting themselves in dire peril of relegation at the end of the season.

Frank Taylor, a former Wolves full-back and coach at Hull City under Frank Buckley, was appointed as Bob McGrory's successor. Known as one of the first "tracksuit" managers, with a reputation for ensuring his players were "90 minutes fit", Taylor inherited a struggling squad, which had grown old together. Also, several of McGrory's star signings on which he had lavished sizable sums had simply flopped. The likes of Jimmy McAlinden, signed from Portsmouth for £7,000 in 1947, and Les Johnston, signed from Celtic for £9,000 in 1949, never made the hoped-for impact. Taylor could not turn things around and the side struggled throughout 1952/53, suffering first Cup humiliation at the hands of Halifax Town and then relegation.

F. TAYLOR

STOKE CITY

Goalkeeper Dennis Herod sees the ball fly across Stoke's penalty area in the 2-1 victory over dark-shirted Wrexham in the FA Cup third-round tie at a fog-bound Victoria Ground in January 1953.

Billy Kiernan scores for Charlton in a 5-1 win over Stoke at a packed Valley in November 1952. Stoke slumped towards the end of the season and were relegated after a final day home defeat by Derby.

Going Down

Humiliation piled upon humiliation as Stoke were relegated in Frank Taylor's first season in charge. Captain Ken Thomson missed a penalty in the last game of a torrid campaign at home to already-relegated Derby on 25th April 1953. Stoke lost 1-2 and finished third from bottom, but had Thomson scored, the draw would have kept the Potters up.

King of the Boothen End

> *Johnny King had the best left foot in the league.*
>
> Stoke captain, Dennis Wilshaw

Johnny King shoots towards the Boothen End net against Middlesbrough in December 1956.

Great Game:
On 13th March 1954 Stoke defeated Bury 6-0 in the Second Division. This remains Stoke's biggest ever away League win. King scored once, with Harry Oscroft netting twice, as did Frank Bowyer. An own goal from Hart completed the thrashing.

FOOTBALL
—STATS—

Johnny King

Name: Johnny King

Born: 1932

Playing Career: 1949–1967

Clubs: Crewe, Stoke, Cardiff, Crewe

Stoke Appearances: 311

Goals: 113

—LEGENDS—

Johnny King

In September 1953 diminutive Johnny King signed from Crewe Alexandra. He formed, along with George "Grace" Kelly, Stoke's "K-Plan", the monicker the press gave the attacking duo. King scored over 100 goals in the Second Division in 311 appearances, making him without doubt Frank Taylor's best signing.

King's wiry build was topped by a light-brown head of wavy hair and he always took the field with his sleeves rolled tightly up above his elbows, ready for work. His magical left foot was capable of deft close control, which enabled him to trick immobile opponents with a nutmeg or a burst of speed. At just 5ft 7in tall, King's low centre of gravity assisted his ability to turn on a sixpence and fool lumbering defenders, who struggled to cope with his skill and verve. He loved playing against big centre-halves and his favourite opponent was Leeds and England's Jack Charlton: "I used to back into him, receive the ball at my feet and then just spin off, leaving him for dead. I loved playing against Leeds," King recalled.

King scored on his home debut against Luton and went on to pass double figures in all but one of the next eight seasons, finishing three times as leading scorer. He notched a hat-trick against Bury on Christmas morning 1955, but it was not until the arrival of one of the most colourful characters ever to don a Stoke shirt, George "Grace" Kelly, in January 1956, that a regular partner emerged. Kelly, a diabetic, also known as "Spider" due to his tall lean frame, forged a dynamic partnership with King. Stoke finished fifth in 1956/57 with the "K-Plan" in action and the pair scored 37 goals between them the following season as Stoke racked up 75 in the League, a total surpassed only once since.

In the final game of the 1959/60 season King grabbed the first goal in a 2-1 win at Ashton Gate, completing a century of goals in all competitions for Stoke, the seventh man to reach this landmark. Thirteen goals in his final season at the Victoria Ground left him in fourth place on the all-time goalscorers list, although he was later overtaken by John Ritchie.

The marathon Cup tie finally came to an end when Tim Coleman netted a somewhat fortuitous winning goal deep into extra time of the fourth replay at Old Trafford. The tie had lasted a record 9 hours and 22 minutes.

When Stoke and Bury were drawn together in the FA Cup third round no one could have foreseen that the two were so evenly matched that they would almost be inseparable. Here a snow-covered Goodison Park plays host to the third game in the five-match series, which finished 3-3 after extra time in front of 2,469 hardy spectators on 17th January 1955.

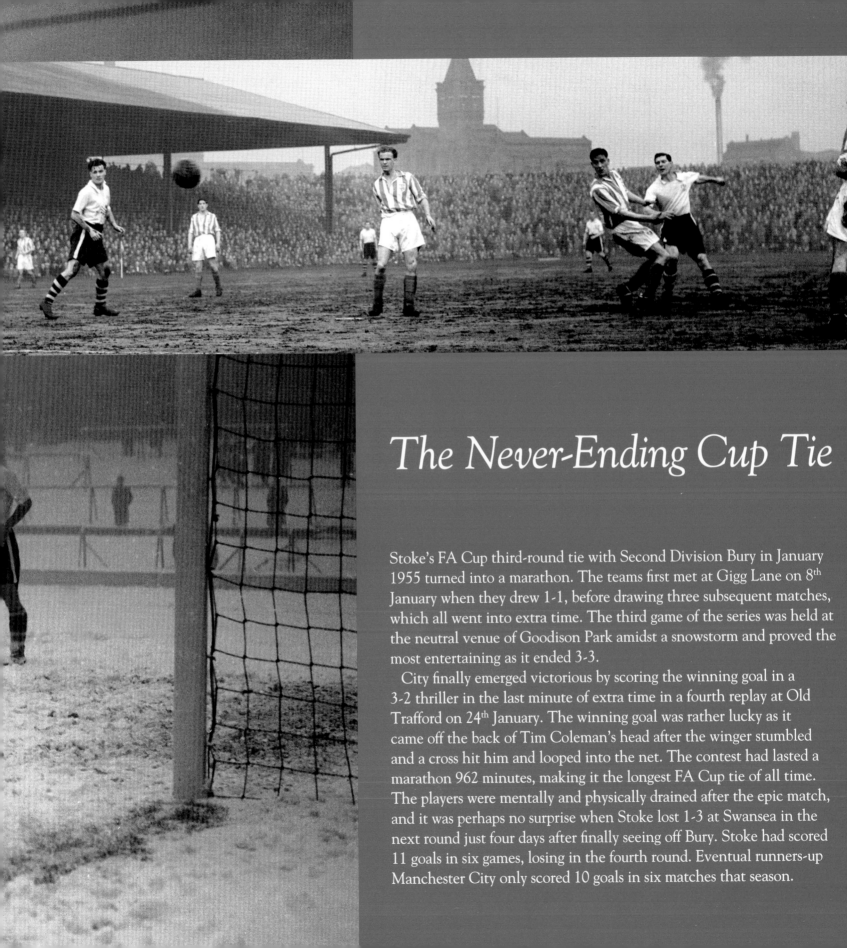

The Never-Ending Cup Tie

Stoke's FA Cup third-round tie with Second Division Bury in January 1955 turned into a marathon. The teams first met at Gigg Lane on 8th January when they drew 1-1, before drawing three subsequent matches, which all went into extra time. The third game of the series was held at the neutral venue of Goodison Park amidst a snowstorm and proved the most entertaining as it ended 3-3.

City finally emerged victorious by scoring the winning goal in a 3-2 thriller in the last minute of extra time in a fourth replay at Old Trafford on 24th January. The winning goal was rather lucky as it came off the back of Tim Coleman's head after the winger stumbled and a cross hit him and looped into the net. The contest had lasted a marathon 962 minutes, making it the longest FA Cup tie of all time. The players were mentally and physically drained after the epic match, and it was perhaps no surprise when Stoke lost 1-3 at Swansea in the next round just four days after finally seeing off Bury. Stoke had scored 11 goals in six games, losing in the fourth round. Eventual runners-up Manchester City only scored 10 goals in six matches that season.

Pre-season Preparations

Jack Marshall (right) welcomes newcomers (left to right) Bobby Cairns, Len Davies, Jack Short and Joe Hutton during pre-season preparations in August 1954.

The 1956 squad face the cameras for their pre-season photocall.

Although the Boothen End had become the home for the majority of Stoke's vociferous supporters, the large open terrace behind the goal at the Town End, little more than a shored-up bank of shale, was the traditional home to families and older supporters, who often mingled with visiting fans, who were not segregated at this time. However, crowds would dwindle as Stoke languished in the Second Division for most of the decade.

Beating Liverpool

The programme from Stoke's 4-3 victory at Liverpool in March 1959, City's last win at Anfield.

A rare photograph from Stoke's first ever victory at Anfield in March 1955. Liverpool had played against Notts County in Nottingham just two nights earlier and so were undoubtedly tired, but Stoke took full advantage to win 4-2. City's scorers were Johnny King (two goals, one a penalty), Johnny Malkin and Harry Oscroft, who netted one of his 21 goals from the left wing that 1954/55 season. Here, Liverpool's legendary Billy Liddell heads narrowly wide of Stoke's goal. The Potters have won only once at Anfield since, in March 1959, winning a magnificent game 4-3.

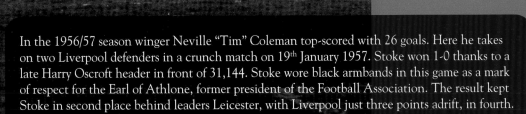

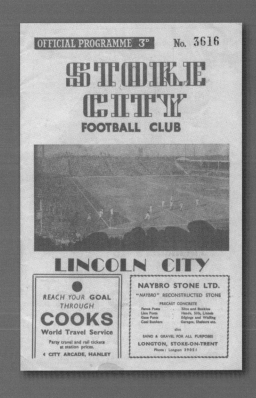

In the 1956/57 season winger Neville "Tim" Coleman top-scored with 26 goals. Here he takes on two Liverpool defenders in a crunch match on 19th January 1957. Stoke won 1-0 thanks to a late Harry Oscroft header in front of 31,144. Stoke wore black armbands in this game as a mark of respect for the Earl of Athlone, former president of the Football Association. The result kept Stoke in second place behind leaders Leicester, with Liverpool just three points adrift, in fourth.

Coleman made his name just a month later when he scored a remarkable seven goals in Stoke's 8-0 hammering of Lincoln City, the most goals ever scored by a winger in a match. At that stage it looked as if Stoke might challenge for promotion, but City would fail to score in six successive games towards the end of the season and ended up in a disappointing fifth position.

Years of Struggle

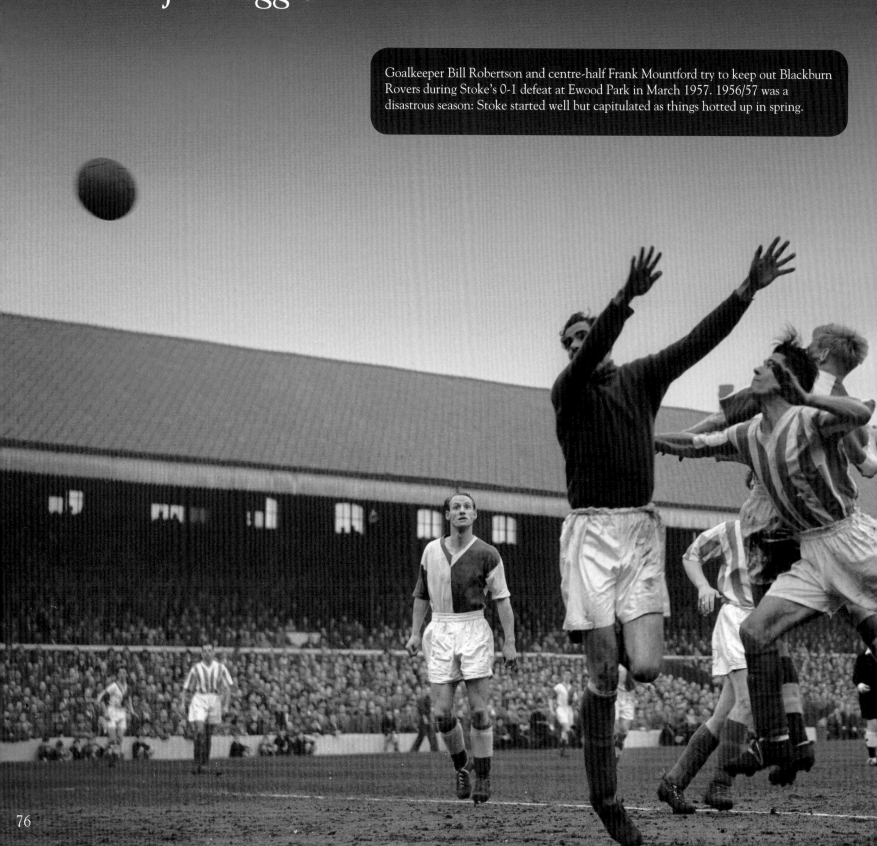

Goalkeeper Bill Robertson and centre-half Frank Mountford try to keep out Blackburn Rovers during Stoke's 0-1 defeat at Ewood Park in March 1957. 1956/57 was a disastrous season: Stoke started well but capitulated as things hotted up in spring.

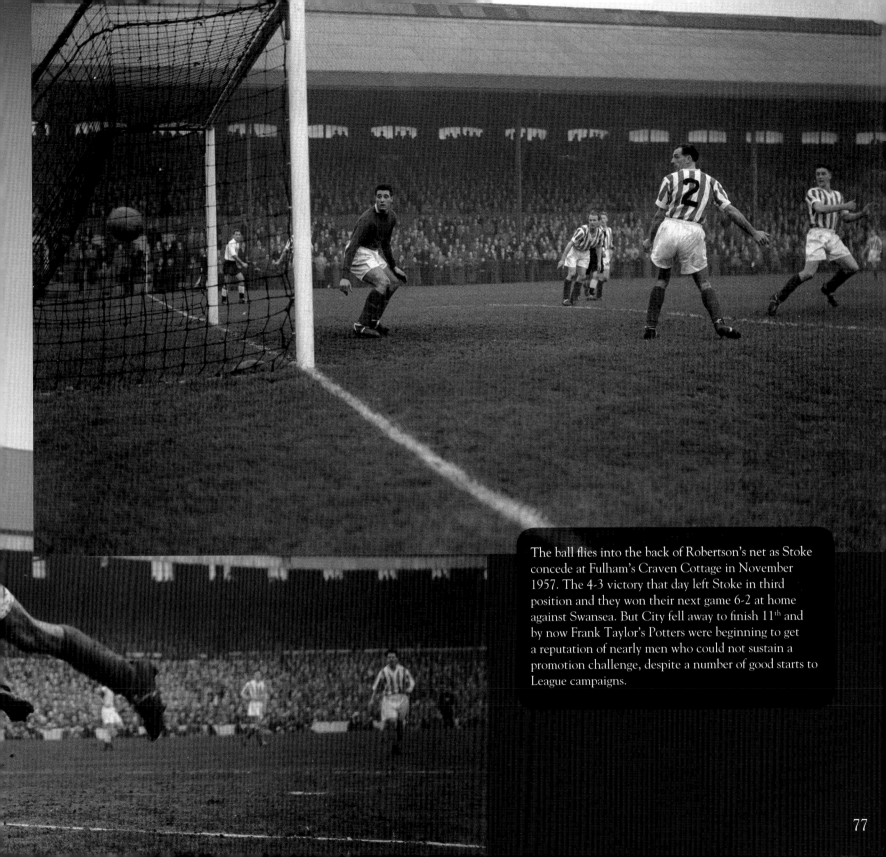

The ball flies into the back of Robertson's net as Stoke concede at Fulham's Craven Cottage in November 1957. The 4-3 victory that day left Stoke in third position and they won their next game 6-2 at home against Swansea. But City fell away to finish 11th and by now Frank Taylor's Potters were beginning to get a reputation of nearly men who could not sustain a promotion challenge, despite a number of good starts to League campaigns.

Striker Andy Graver – known as "Homing Pigeon" because of his tendency to return to Lincolnshire – signed from Lincoln City for £11,000 in November 1955 after Frank Taylor's pursuit of Blackpool's Stan Mortensen came to nothing. Graver was not a success and scored only 14 goals in 42 games for Stoke before moving on to Boston United in April 1957. Here he is thwarted by Bristol Rovers' goalkeeper at the Victoria Ground in December 1956. Graver did have the last laugh on this day, however, as he scored the winning goal in a 2-1 victory. Interestingly, the old gasometer that stood behind the corner of the Butler Street Stand and the Boothen End can be seen poking into shot from this angle.

The other half of Stoke's "K-Plan", George "Grace" Kelly, smashes home a goal against Grimsby at the Victoria Ground in October 1957. Kelly scored twice in a 4-1 victory. The former Aberdeen striker netted 35 goals in 67 games at Stoke before joining Cardiff City. Kelly and fellow striker Johnny King were more than strike partners. After they retired from football the pair came together to play doubles tennis and almost qualified for the Wimbledon championships.

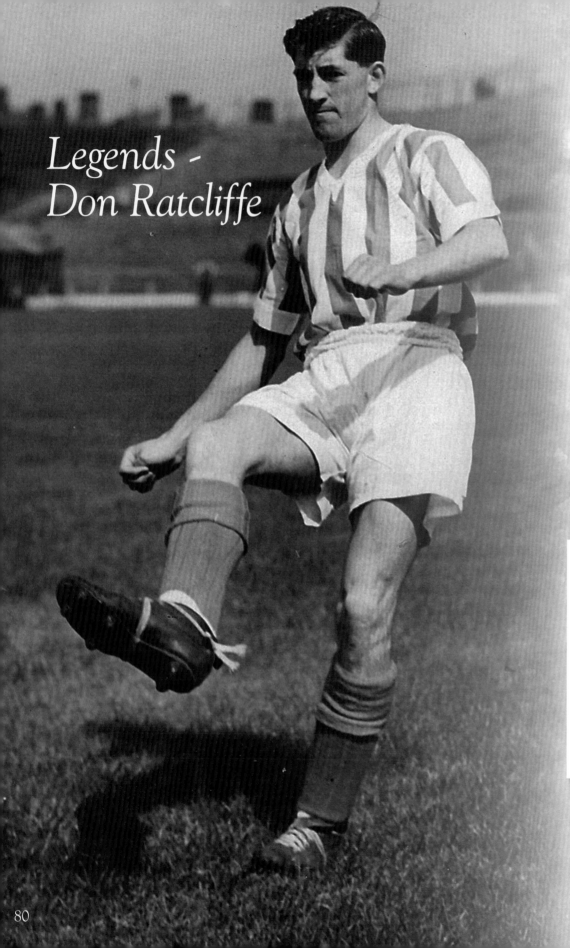

Legends - Don Ratcliffe

Taylor introduced more local players into his squad in the latter part of the 1950s. In December 1954 tyro midfielder Don Ratcliffe made his debut against Bury and soon became a firm fan favourite for his perpetual motion style. "Ratter", as he was known, never stopped running and once played a long pass down the wing, saw no one was bothering to chase it, hared after it himself and caught up with it by the corner flag. He would also, it was often joked, run out of the gates at the end of the ground if they were left open, as he just ran and ran and ran. Ratcliffe was blessed with no little skill, though, and scored 19 goals in 260 games for the Potters before joining Middlesbrough for £27,500 in 1963. That came after new manager Tony Waddington had joked he could make Ratcliffe the first £100,000 footballer as he could sell him for £10,000 for each of the 10 positions in which Don had played in the Stoke first team.

Don Ratcliffe's contract with Stoke from 1961 to 1962 shows he earned the princely sum of £16 per week, plus £6 10s when playing in the first team.

Stoke's apprentices try to thaw the frozen Victoria Ground pitch, overseen by Don Ratcliffe (left). Braziers such as the one "Ratter" is warming his hands on were often used to thaw the playing surface in winter, while in summer sheep were sometimes used to "cut" the grass.

Promotion Missed Again

Goalkeeper Bill Robertson makes a flying save at Huddersfield in September 1957 in a game which Stoke lost 0-1. Taylor finally lost patience with the former Chelsea custodian after a mistake cost City points and Robertson was replaced by Wilf Hall for most of the rest of the season after this defeat. Stoke were second at Christmas but won only four of their last 13 games, which included four successive home defeats, thus throwing promotion away.

It wasn't all bad, though! Here, a mistake by Dave Groombridge, the Orient keeper, lets in George Kelly (just visible over the shoulder of Stoke's number 11, Harry Oscroft) to fire home the second goal in Stoke's 2-0 victory at Brisbane Road in August 1957.

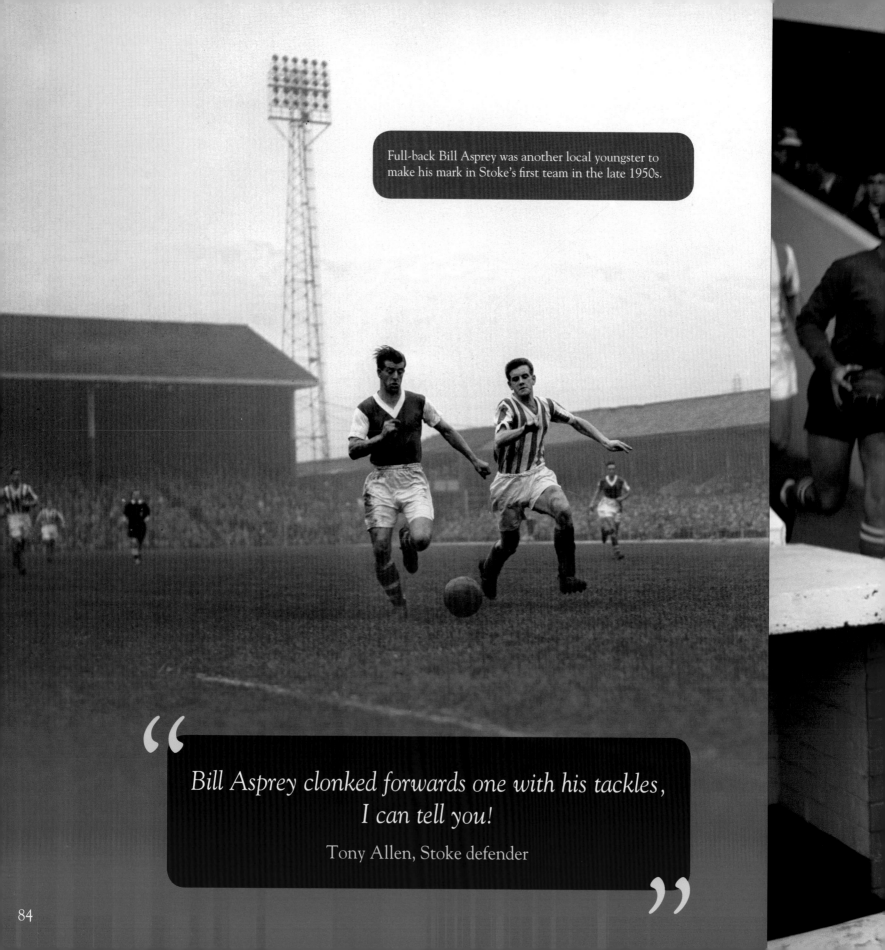

Full-back Bill Asprey was another local youngster to make his mark in Stoke's first team in the late 1950s.

Bill Asprey clonked forwards one with his tackles, I can tell you!

Tony Allen, Stoke defender

–LEGENDS–

Bill Asprey

Bill Asprey was a sturdy defender, blessed with a powerful shot, which led to him scoring more than his fair share of goals. Indeed, he once bagged a hat-trick playing as an emergency centre-forward in January 1961. Asprey was ever present in 1958/59, 1961/62 and the promotion season of 1962/63, making 101 consecutive appearances in the process. Tall for a full-back at 6ft 1in, Asprey became captain in 1964. He moved on to Oldham in 1967 and then coached Coventry, Wolves and West Brom before managing Oxford United and then returning to Stoke as first-team coach under Richie Barker and then manager in his own right. Sadly, although he kept Stoke in the First Division in 1984 Asprey couldn't stop relegation the following season and he was sacked part-way through.

FOOTBALL –STATS–

Bill Asprey

Name: Bill Asprey

Born: 1936

Playing Career: 1953–1968

Clubs: Stoke, Oldham, Stockport

Stoke Appearances: 341

Goals: 26

Asprey runs out of the Victoria Ground tunnel after the construction of the new main stand in 1962.

MOMENT OF MADNESS...

By FRANK McGHEE

Stoke 2, Aston Villa 0

ONE moment of madness shoved Aston Villa, last year's Wembley winners, out of the Cup at Wolverhampton yesterday.

One tragically stupid blunder by right half Vic Crowe ... and their dream of another money-spinning success was stone dead.

It happened in the fifty-fifth minute of this third round second replay. The score was 0-0 and looked certain to stay that way.

Then over from the Stoke left wing floated a high, harmless cross, swinging gently away from the penalty area.

No Stoke forward could have reached it. Crowe could — and did. But for some reason best known to himself he reached with his hand and flicked the ball on its way!

A flagrant penalty — so glaring that the crowd were stunned into silence.

All Crowe could do was clap his hands to his red head in anguish as his opposite number, Scot Bob Cairns, smashed the ball past Nigel Sims.

Villa were never in the game after that. They simply surrendered.

You couldn't recognise the old firm which played with such fiery spirit throughout last season's competition.

On an ice rink of a pitch, they were hesitant, uneasy.

The speed of tackle normally shown in defence was missing; the razor-edged menace of the attack was blunted.

And Stoke, always the faster, neater outfit, clinched the fourth round game against Middlesbrough four minutes from time.

Centre forward Dennis Wilshaw drew the defence and slipped over a perfect cross.

Out go the Cup holders

For once it was not Stoke on the end of a Cup shock when, in January 1958, they knocked FA Cup-holders Aston Villa out in a second replay. A capacity crowd of 45,800 packed into the Victoria Ground for the original tie, which ended 1-1 after George Kelly tapped in an equalizer midway through the second half, following Peter McParland's opener.

At Villa Park the replay proved riotously entertaining. Coleman opened the scoring for Stoke after 90 seconds and Kelly added a second on the half-hour. Villa fought back to take a 3-2 lead, but Oscroft netted with three minutes to go to force a second replay. This time Stoke triumphed 2-0 at neutral Molineux with Coleman and diminutive midfielder Bobby Cairns netting the goals. Cairns' penalty followed Crowe's handball on the line and secured a deserved and famous victory point.

Striker Dennis Wilshaw – Stoke's last amateur player.

Cup Heroics

Stoke's reward for defeating Cup-holders Villa was a home draw against Middlesbrough and their goalscoring phenomenon Brian Clough. But the tyro striker didn't have it all his own way. Despite scoring the opening goal, Clough was overshadowed by elder statesman Dennis Wilshaw, who had recently signed for Stoke from Wolves and was nearing his 32nd birthday. Wilshaw scored his first Stoke goals to net a hat-trick, which won the game 3-1 for the Potters, and kicked Clough up the backside to boot!

Four inches of snow was cleared by volunteers that morning to allow the game to go ahead and 43,756 witnessed Wilshaw's treble, made up of two tap-ins into an empty net before half-time and the *coup de grâce*, a firm shot from a King pass with 15 minutes to go. Having scored a hat-trick, Wilshaw took the opportunity to whack the prone Clough's backside after the whippersnapper had been fouled and was hauling himself up from the frozen turf. Luckily the referee was looking the other way and Clough went into a huff and didn't threaten Stoke's goal again.

Wilshaw was a former England international who had once scored five goals against Scotland at Wembley. An amateur throughout his career, Wilshaw was a qualified maths teacher who trained in his spare time. Sadly his stay at his hometown club of Stoke was foreshortened when his leg was broken by a bad tackle by Bill Thompson at Newcastle. But Wilshaw left his indelible mark on the club by coaching the Stoke-on-Trent boys' team, containing the likes of Denis Smith, Bill Bentley and Jackie Marsh, which won consecutive English Schools' Trophies in 1962 and 1963. He was also the man to spark an idea in new manager Tony Waddington's mind when, as he hobbled around the training ground on crutches, Wilshaw commented that only one man could truly revive the fortunes of Stoke City: Stanley Matthews. The rest was history.

ABOVE: The Stoke team which knocked out both Aston Villa and Middlesbrough from the FA Cup in 1958, and then played under floodlights for the first time.

In 1959 floodlights appeared at the Victoria Ground, following their introduction at many other clubs. Radnički (Yugoslavia) and Essen (West Germany) were beaten 3-0 and 5-0 in floodlit friendlies before intrigued supporters.

Stoke welcomed Austria's oldest club First Vienna to the Victoria Ground in 1959 for a floodlit friendly. The game ended 1-1.

FOOTBALL –STATS–

Tony Allen

Name: Tony Allen

Born: 1939

Playing Career: 1957–1971

Clubs: Stoke, Bury

Stoke Appearances: 473

Goals: 4

STOKE CITY FOOTBALL CLUB

★ ★ ★

STOKE CITY
versus
FIRST VIENNA
FOOTBALL CLUB OF AUSTRIA

VICTORIA GROUND
SATURDAY, 14th FEBRUARY, 1959
Kick-off 3-15 p.m.

★ ★ ★

Souvenir Programme · Price Threepence

–LEGENDS–

Tony Allen

One of the bright sparks on the Stoke City horizon at the end of the 1950s was new England international defender Tony Allen. The blond-haired full-back stood out because of both his blond locks and his ability to read the game, which brought him to the attention of England coach Walter Winterbottom, who was looking to give young players their chance after a disastrous World Cup in Sweden in 1958. Allen won three caps at the age of just 19 in the autumn of 1959 against Wales, Sweden and Northern Ireland.

Allen did not have it all his own way, though. In a 2-4 home defeat by Blackburn, Allen had rings run round him by England winger Bryan Douglas. "I was that ashamed I didn't get the bus home. I walked," he said. Allen worked hard on his game and became a vital brick in Tony Waddington's "Wall" as City established themselves back in the top flight in the 1960s.

Ever present from March 1960 to March 1963, Allen played in 148 consecutive games for Stoke, setting a new record, which still stands today. Later in his career, as his pace dwindled, he switched from full-back to centre-half, performing with distinction, before moving on to Bury in 1970.

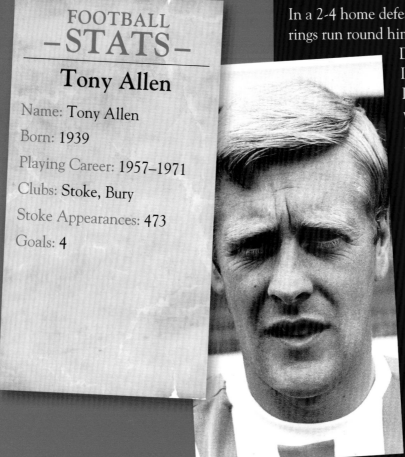

Goals and Excitement, but No Cigar

Stoke were renowned for scoring goals, but all too often conceded just as many, as happened in this see-saw game with League leaders Cardiff, which ended 4-4 in November 1959. Stoke led by two goals at 4-2, only for the home side to peg City back in the last 10 minutes. The disappointing draw set the tone for yet another in-and-out season.

Bill Robertson both hurt his back and broke two ribs in a collision with Joe Bonson, who scored Cardiff's third goal. The injured 36-year-old keeper would not play for Stoke again.

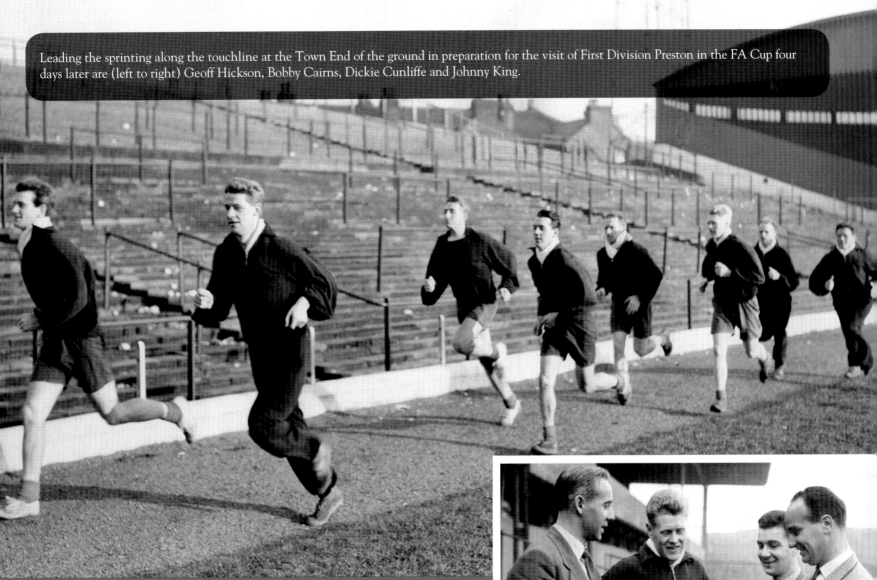

Leading the sprinting along the touchline at the Town End of the ground in preparation for the visit of First Division Preston in the FA Cup four days later are (left to right) Geoff Hickson, Bobby Cairns, Dickie Cunliffe and Johnny King.

Cup Preparations:
Tuesday 5th January 1960

Because of Stoke's continued failure to get close to winning promotion back to the First Division, by the 1959/60 season City's average gate had fallen below 10,000 for the first time since the club re-entered the League after the First World War. Doom and gloom encumbered the Victoria Ground and it spelt the end for likeable, but ultimately unsuccessful, manager, Frank Taylor, who departed in May 1960.

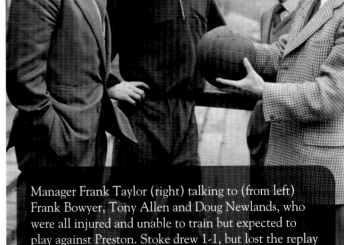

Manager Frank Taylor (right) talking to (from left) Frank Bowyer, Tony Allen and Doug Newlands, who were all injured and unable to train but expected to play against Preston. Stoke drew 1-1, but lost the replay at Deepdale 1-3.

The Old Crocks
1960-70

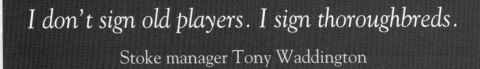

> *I don't sign old players. I sign thoroughbreds.*
>
> Stoke manager Tony Waddington

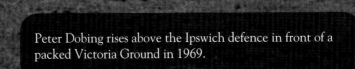

Peter Dobing rises above the Ipswich defence in front of a packed Victoria Ground in 1969.

1960 Tony Waddington is appointed as manager of Stoke City. Stoke thrash Plymouth 9-0, the club's largest ever margin of victory in the Football League. 1961 Stanley Matthews returns to Stoke aged 46, trebling crowds in an instant. 1962 "Old Crocks" Eddie Stuart, Eddie Clamp, Dennis Viollet and Jimmy McIlroy sign. Matthews becomes the oldest goalscorer, aged 45 years 349 days, in FA Cup history when he nets past Gordon Banks in a 5-2 win over Leicester. 1963 Stoke draw 2-2 with Real Madrid in a special centenary celebration match. Stoke win the Second Division championship. 1964 City lose the two-legged League Cup final 3-4 to Leicester City. Stoke thrash Ipswich 9-1, their largest ever First Division victory. 1965 Harry Burrows signs from Aston Villa. Stanley Matthews plays in the First Division aged 50, bids farewell to football and is knighted by the Queen. 1967 Gordon Banks signs for Stoke. 1969 Pelé's Santos play a prestige friendly at Stoke and win 3-2. The famous homegrown defence of Marsh, Pejic, Bloor and Smith first plays together against Sunderland. Tony Allen plays the last of his 473 games for Stoke. 1970 Terrace accident on the Boothen End injures 60.

A New Era Begins

New manager Tony Waddington was appointed in June 1960. "Waddo", as he became universally known, was aged only 35 and had been invalided out of his playing career with Manchester United after picking up a knee injury during service in the Royal Navy. He had been first-team coach at Stoke under Taylor and was the Board's unanimous choice to succeed the departed manager.

Don Ratcliffe and Dennis Viollet leap in time under the watchful eye of trainer Dougie Brown in the players' gym under the Boothen End.

Bill Asprey cracks in the opening goal in the first minute, following a sharp turn to begin the avalanche of goals.

Plymouth's captain Fincham is left flat-out after scoring an own goal.

Great Game:
17th December 1960, Stoke 9-0 Plymouth.

Waddington struggled to make an impact in his first season, but on 17th December 1960 his Stoke team suddenly went goal crazy and beat Plymouth 9-0. It was totally unexpected as Stoke had failed to score in either of their previous two matches and Stoke stood in a lowly 17th position, while Plymouth were eighth and had won the return fixture 3-1 on the opening day of the season. None of the 6,479 hardy Stoke fans could have foreseen such an incredible performance. Stoke had not won at the Victoria Ground since 1st October and there was talk of a goal famine as 20 League games had thus far only yielded 18 goals.

What followed was a whirlwind of goals as Asprey, playing as an emergency centre-forward, opened the scoring in the first minute with a sharp shot from eight yards, then Fincham scored an own goal while attempting to stop Bentley's goalbound effort. King rattled in a third before half-time, but the floodgates opened in the second half. Asprey prodded a Wilshaw free-kick between Barnsley's legs in the Plymouth goal to make it four. Wilshaw hammered in off the underside of the bar on 69 minutes and King lashed in from 22 yards to make it 6-0 on 77 minutes. The seventh came from Ratcliffe just three minutes later and the eighth from King, who completed his hat-trick by flicking an Asprey centre over the heads of two defenders on the goal line. The final goal, when Ratcliffe prodded in a King effort, which was spinning towards goal after being deflected, made it 9-0, Stoke's biggest ever margin of victory in League football. Plymouth were crushed and mesmerized as Stoke tore them to shreds with some blistering moves. It was a massacre and things were now on the up.

Waddington Wall

Waddington's first innovation was to protect his back-four with two defensive midfield players and bring in ageing stars who had been proven winners at successful clubs, but were now being moved on. The likes of Wolves defenders Eddie Stuart and Eddie Clamp, Everton's goalkeeper Jimmy O'Neill and Blackpool striker Jackie Mudie allowed Stoke to finish eighth in 1961/62, after avoiding relegation by only one point during the previous campaign. Momentum was gathering.

Jimmy O'Neill was Tony Waddington's first signing when he became Stoke City manager in 1960. Waddo paid £2,000 for the Everton keeper who had won 17 caps for the Republic of Ireland, persuading O'Neill to join Stoke rather than fellow Second Division club Liverpool by buying a cooker for Mrs O'Neill. Jimmy was small for a goalkeeper at 5ft 10in, but had a reputation as both a shot-stopper and someone who commanded the penalty area and claimed crosses. He kept 48 clean sheets in his 49 games for Stoke and missed just two matches in three seasons, including the promotion-winning campaign of 1962/63.

Eddie Clamp became Stanley Matthews' minder. A tough-tackling, almost psychopathic cruncher, Clamp was good enough to play for England during the 1958 World Cup, while he was with Wolves. Waddington brought him to Stoke, after an abortive spell at Arsenal, for £35,000 in September 1962. Clamp christened Matthews "Uncle" and would warn the elder statesman's full-back before the game kicked off that if they kicked Stan then Eddie would exact a terrible revenge. If Stan was fouled then Clamp would snarl: "If you do that again you'll wake up in hospital." He wasn't joking. At Cardiff, Clamp once headbutted opposing player Colin Webster because seven years earlier, while playing for Manchester United, Webster had ended Stoke full-back George Bourne's promising career at the age of 23 by breaking his leg in a bad tackle. "Eddie was mad," confirms then-trainer Frank Mountford. "He never used to turn up for training and we would have to send someone to fetch him from his home in Wolverhampton. He soon realized that if he continued to not turn up we'd fetch him and he wouldn't have to pay to get to training!"

> *I brought nine players back behind the ball when the opposition had it and played the wingers deep. It wasn't pretty, but it was effective.*
>
> Tony Waddington

Eddie Stuart's first day at work at Stoke after signing from Wolves in July 1962. (Above left) Stuart challenges Don Ratcliffe for a header in training, (above centre) is dunked by his new team-mates in the Victoria Ground baths, (above right) has lunch with Bobby Howitt, who he would quickly replace as skipper, and (below) leaves the players' entrance and signs autographs for his new fans. Stuart was one of Waddington's "Old Crocks" as he had won three League titles in his time with Wolves and had just turned 31 when he joined Stoke for £8,000. He moved on to Tranmere for £4,000 in 1966.

Stan Returns

A packed Boothen End and the national press admire Stan's first corner in his second spell at Stoke.

Stan is besieged by autograph-hunting fans after the 3-0 victory over Huddersfield on his return.

October 1961 proved the turning point for Stoke City under Tony Waddington when he secured the return to the Victoria Ground of Stanley Matthews. The "Wizard of Dribble" was now 46 years old and had barely played for Blackpool in the preceding season, but Waddington knew he could galvanize the sleeping giant in the Potteries by capturing Stan. It worked. And how. Matthews signed on television in front of the BBC's *Sportsview* cameras and 35,000 excited Stoke fans packed the Victoria Ground to welcome the 46-year-old winger home. The previous home game's attendance had been just 8,000.

One man and his adoring public: Stan Matthews in front of the packed Town End during his return match against Huddersfield. Matthews' fairytale return attracted huge interest and revitalized the flagging fortunes of Stoke City almost overnight.

The Two Sides of Stanley Matthews

The loneliness of training on the beach near his home in Blackpool – Matthews' dedication to fitness, including only drinking tomato juice on Mondays to get the toxins out of his body so he could play a better game of football, was the reason behind his incredible longevity in the game.

RIGHT: The other, far more public, side of Stan Matthews. The much-loved public face of Stoke City's revival is here seen with ball-juggling act the Balladinis at Blackpool's Tower Ballroom circus. The press, radio and television loved Stan and he obliged with plenty of "stunts" to keep them happy. Stan had by now become the most popular sportsman in the country, and was famous around the world, especially after turning the tide of the first FA Cup final to be televised, in 1953, when he prompted Stan Mortensen to score a hat-trick and then crossed for Bill Perry to net the winner as Blackpool came from 1-3 down to clinch a magnificent 4-3 triumph in the "Matthews' final".

97

Record-breaking Stan!

Three steps to FA Cup glory: 1. Stan rounds England goalkeeper Gordon Banks …

3. … then Matthews is mobbed at the end of the game, which Stoke won 5-2.

2. … then celebrates after slotting the ball home to become the oldest ever FA-Cup goalscorer, just 16 days before his 46th birthday …

Another episode in the Stan Matthews fairytale came when Stan scored against Gordon Banks in a 5-2 victory over First Division Leicester in an FA Cup third-round replay on 15th January 1962. A crowd of 38,515 witnessed Matthews become the oldest man to score in the FA Cup. The magic moment arrived in the 23rd minute when a sharp ball downfield found Stan one-on-one with full-back Maurice Norman with acres of wing space to play with. Matthews raced past Norman like a gazelle, despite being 20 years older than the fresh-faced left-back. As Banks advanced, Matthews aimed a perfect low shot inside the far post, which went in crisply off the woodwork. The crowd went wild; "the biggest wave of cheering at the Victoria Ground for years," cried the *Sentinel*. It was the first of five goals, with Allen, Bullock, Nibloe and Thompson the other scorers. Matthews earned a standing ovation from the 38,525 crowd at the end, many of whom were beside themselves with jubilation and mobbed him as he left the pitch.

The Old Crocks

Tony Waddington's "Old Crocks" earned their nickname because they were stars released from big clubs and generally aged over 28. The likes of Stan Matthews, Eddie Stuart, Eddie Clamp, Jimmy McIlroy, Jackie Mudie and Dennis Viollet arrived within a year of each other as Waddington built a team to challenge for promotion in 1962/63.

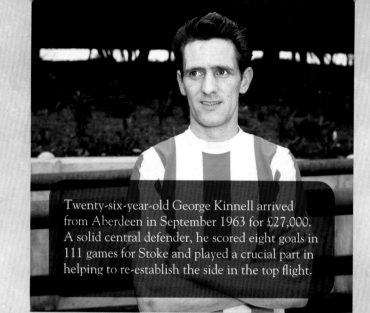

Twenty-six-year-old George Kinnell arrived from Aberdeen in September 1963 for £27,000. A solid central defender, he scored eight goals in 111 games for Stoke and played a crucial part in helping to re-establish the side in the top flight.

> " *A violet by a mossy stone, half-hidden from the eye. Fair as a star when only one is shining in the sky. He was just there on the spot when needed.* "
>
> Commentator Stuart Hall

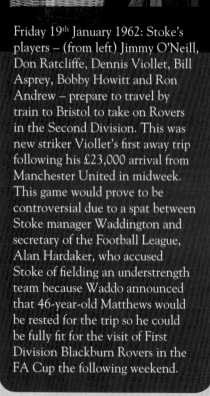

Friday 19th January 1962: Stoke's players – (from left) Jimmy O'Neill, Don Ratcliffe, Dennis Viollet, Bill Asprey, Bobby Howitt and Ron Andrew – prepare to travel by train to Bristol to take on Rovers in the Second Division. This was new striker Viollet's first away trip following his £23,000 arrival from Manchester United in midweek. This game would prove to be controversial due to a spat between Stoke manager Waddington and secretary of the Football League, Alan Hardaker, who accused Stoke of fielding an understrength team because Waddo announced that 46-year-old Matthews would be rested for the trip so he could be fully fit for the visit of First Division Blackburn Rovers in the FA Cup the following weekend.

Dennis Viollet signs from Manchester United for £22,000 – another transfer coup for Tony Waddington.

FOOTBALL – STATS –

Dennis Viollet

Name: Dennis Viollet

Born: 1933

Died: 1999

Playing Career: 1949–1967

Clubs: Manchester United, Stoke

Stoke Appearances: 207

Goals: 66

–LEGENDS–

Dennis Viollet

Dennis Viollet, one of the original Busby Babes, formed a devastating partnership for Stoke with Jimmy McIlroy and Jackie Mudie. Despite numbering over 90 years between them, they pulverized opposing defences with quality football as City won promotion to the First Division. Viollet's 5ft 8in height and 11st frame gave him a frail, almost ghoulish appearance, which belied his stamina and, in particular, his skill. The most common word used to describe Viollet's play is "ghost" – whether it be his appearance or his manner of beating defenders. As an accurate passer with a beguiling body swerve, he used his stealth and skill to turn half-chances into goals. Aged 28 when he arrived at the Victoria Ground, Viollet was actually in his prime, although the papers insisted he was another of the band of "Old Crocks" to arrive at the Victoria Ground.

His contribution soon kick-started Stoke into becoming the form team in the division and a run of just one defeat in 13 games, with 23-goal Viollet starring alongside Mudie and McIlroy, ensured Stoke returned to the First Division as champions in 1962/63.

The following season, after the acquisition of inside-left George Eastham, Waddington pulled off a positional master stroke. He recognized that Viollet had lost a bit of pace and withdrew him into midfield, where his razor-sharp football brain could wreak havoc.

Many critics and fans believed that Viollet attained even greater heights at Stoke than at United and he was awarded a testimonial in May 1967, before retiring to the United States.

Jimmy McIlroy

Despite being better remembered as a player with another club, Burnley – with whom he won a League championship in 1960 and at whose Turf Moor ground he has a stand named after him – Jimmy McIlroy etched himself firmly into Stoke fans' hearts. After clinching his signature in controversial circumstances when egotistical Burnley Chairman Bob Lord transfer-listed McIlroy without the midfielder's knowledge, Tony Waddington eschewed the idea that McIlroy was another of his "Old Crocks" saying: "I don't sign old players. I sign thoroughbreds."

A scheming player blessed with an ability to open up a defence with one, beautifully angled, pass, McIlroy won 55 Northern Irish caps, 34 consecutively, which was then a record. Perfectly balanced, McIlroy's tantalizing footwork made him a crowd favourite at Stoke too. McIlroy's best season was 1963/64 when he scored 13 goals to finish as third highest goalscorer as Stoke re-established themselves in the top flight and won a League Cup runners-up medal to boot. McIlroy joined Oldham in 1965 and later became a journalist. He was awarded the MBE in the 2011 New Year's Honours list for his services to football and charity.

Jimmy McIlroy beams as he joins Tony Waddington's Stoke revolution.

FOOTBALL –STATS–

Jimmy McIlroy

Name: Jimmy McIlroy

Born: 1931

Playing Career: 1950–1967

Clubs: Burnley, Stoke, Oldham

Stoke Appearances: 116

Goals: 19

1963: The Big Freeze

Stoke Chairman Albert Henshall demonstrates his vision of how an aluminum sheet over the pitch when heated would thaw the ground and allow play all season round at the Victoria Ground. Can't think why it didn't catch on!

The winter of 1963 was the worst in living memory and Stoke did not manage to play a game between Boxing Day and 2nd March. Not for the want of trying! Here, on 16th January, ground staff try to clear several feet of snow off the Victoria Ground and Boothen End to keep the following day's game on. They didn't manage it.

Despite the incredible weather, Stoke were in the top three of the Second Division for the entire season and were top on 20th April. But three successive defeats saw City wobble and both Chelsea and Sunderland looked strong. So City's visit to Stamford Bridge on 11th May proved a pivotal game. Stan Matthews played a blinder and gave young Chelsea full-back Ron Harris the runaround. Jimmy O'Neill and Tony Allen were also outstanding in defence, and Jimmy McIlroy netted the vital winning goal. Stoke won 1-0. Now City just needed two more points from their last three games to clinch promotion.

CHELSEA

Colours—Shirts: Royal Blue (White Facings).   Shorts: White.
Stockings: Blue; Blue and White tops.

(Goal)
Bonetti
1

(Right-back)
Shellito
2

(Left-back)
McCreadie
3

(Right-half)
Venables
4

(Centre-half)
Mortimore
5

(Left-half)
Harris (R.)
6

(Outside-right)
Murray
7

(Inside-right)
Tambling
8

(Centre-forward)
Bridges
9

(Inside-left)
Moore
10

(Outside-left)
Blunstone
11

Referee :
Mr. A. W. SPARLING
(Grimsby)

Linesmen :
Mr. G. W. T. DAVIS
(Romford)
(Red Flag)

Mr. E. HARVEY
(Warboys, Hants)
(Yellow Flag)

11 **Ratcliffe**
(Outside-left)

10 **McIlroy**
(Inside-left)

9 **Mudie**
(Centre-forward)

8 **Viollet**
(Inside-right)

7 **Matthews**
(Outside-right)

6 **Skeels**
(Left-half)

5 **Stuart**
(Centre-half)

4 **Clamp**
(Right-half)

3 **Allen**
(Left-back)

2 **Asprey**
(Right-back)

1 **O'Neill**
(Goal)

STOKE CITY

Colours—Shirts: Red and White Stripes.   Shorts: White.
Stockings: Red, with White Tops.

7

LEAGUE
CHAMPIONS
1954-55

Chelsea
Football Club

Stamford Bridge Grounds, London SW6

FOOTBALL LEAGUE—DIVISION II   SEASON 1962-63
CHELSEA
v
STOKE CITY
Saturday, 11th May, 1963   Kick-off 3 p.m.

Official Programme   6D   The right of admission to grounds is reserved.

The teams from Stoke's vital 1-0 victory at Chelsea in May 1963.

Centenary and Promotion Celebrations!

On 24th April 1963 Stoke played a Centenary Celebration match against five-time European Champions Real Madrid at the Victoria Ground. The match was watched by almost 45,000 supporters who witnessed a 2-2 draw in a match full of stars, which was fitting for the occasion.

Captain for the night Stanley Matthews shakes hands with Real Madrid's Alfredo Di Stéfano.

Matthews takes on the massed Real defence.

Real's Ruiz hits the woodwork from close range with Jimmy O'Neill beaten, but Stoke managed a 2-2 draw against mighty Madrid.

City Clinch Promotion

Stoke defeated Luton Town 2-0 on 18th May 1963 to gain the two points that ensured both promotion and the Second Division championship were secured simultaneously. Poetically, the clinching second goal was scored by 48-year-old Stanley Matthews, who hared onto Jimmy McIlroy's through ball and slotted past keeper Ron Baynham.

The players celebrate in the main stand of the Victoria Ground, enjoying the adulation of the crowd who had invaded the muddy pitch in their thousands.

Don Ratcliffe throws himself into the fray as Stoke seek promotion against Luton.

The two goalscorers, Stan Matthews (left) and Jackie Mudie, celebrate with some well-deserved champagne. Matthews was voted Football Writers' Association's Footballer of the Year for his part in Stoke's triumph. He became the first man to win it twice, the second time 15 years after the first, and remains the oldest winner at 48 years of age.

–LEGENDS–

Peter Dobing

Peter Dobing was English football's first country gentleman. His beloved leisure pursuits were fishing for trout in the River Tern, often with Stoke player-coach Harry Gregg, or roaming the fields near his Market Drayton home, making up the numbers in shooting parties. Although he declared that his secret ambition had always been to become a poacher when he retired from playing football, he claimed never to have had a bloodlust: "I never actually kill anything. That's something I could just not do."

Sartorially elegant in three-piece suits and a hat, Dobing would never be seen without his beloved pipe, belying the Swinging Sixties that the rest of the country was living through. "You get far more satisfaction out of a pipe. I used to smoke cigarettes but now I never touch them." He became something of a trendsetter in the Stoke dressing room with three team-mates, Greenhoff, Ritchie and Stevenson, and even trainer Frank Mountford, taking up smoking a pipe. Unfortunately for Dobing his disciples took their lessons too literally and availed themselves of his tobacco too!

Dobing's *Boys' Own* looks and classic inside-forward style of play harked back to an era fast disappearing. He was a cultured ball player whose main ability was to see passes and execute them devastatingly. He could score too. In 1966/67 and 1967/68 Dobing finished as Stoke's leading scorer, on the second occasion level with Harry Burrows. Dobing finally won the Boothen Enders over with a superb display against Leeds and England defender Jack Charlton at the Victoria Ground in 1967. Dobing ran rings round Charlton and scored a hat-trick as Stoke won a tempestuous match 3-2.

Dobing captained Stoke to the League Cup final, scoring three goals en route. On the Monday before the final he pulled a thigh muscle and almost missed out on his place in the team. Still restricted in his movement on the day, Dobing was determined to play after tasting defeat with Blackburn in the FA Cup final at Wembley in 1960. Eventually the injuries took their toll and Dobing quit the game after breaking his leg for a third time as a Stoke player in 1973.

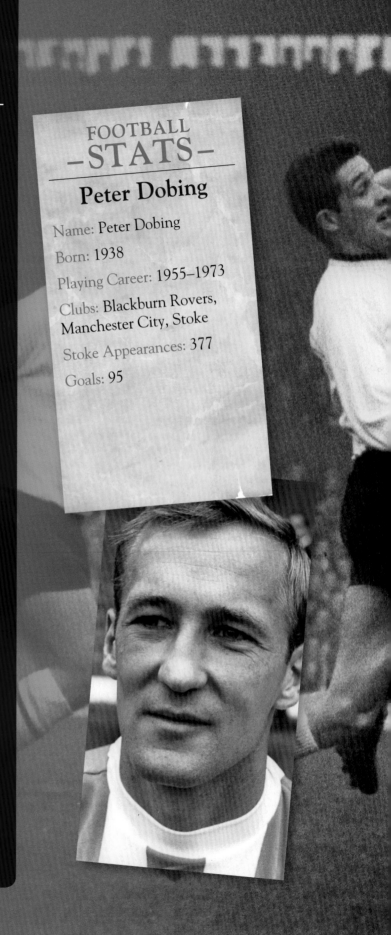

FOOTBALL –STATS–

Peter Dobing

Name: Peter Dobing

Born: 1938

Playing Career: 1955–1973

Clubs: Blackburn Rovers, Manchester City, Stoke

Stoke Appearances: 377

Goals: 95

Peter Dobing's "agent" (his baby son Anthony) negotiates Stoke's new signing's contract. Dobing arrived at Stoke in 1963 and would go on to become captain during a 10-year stay.

Dobing had an often uneasy relationship with the Boothen End. An artist with the ball he was sometimes perceived to be "lazy". But then would come fantastic goals or bursts of scoring, which got him back in Stoke fans' good books. Here Dobing, beating Smith and Talbut to the ball, lashes home Stoke's fourth goal in front of over 37,000 fans as Stoke draw 4-4 at home with Burnley in November 1963. It was one of 16 goals Dobing scored in his first season at Stoke.

Dobing was no angel at times. In 1970 he limped out of an FA disciplinary hearing with a then-record nine-week ban for exceeding disciplinary points again. The ban was academic though as Dobing was already out for months thanks to a broken leg picked up in a crunching tackle with Ipswich's Mick Mills.

Ladies' Day

STOKE CITY F.C.
Back row, L to R: F. Mountford (Trainer), Ritchie, Kinnell, Asprey, Leslie, Setters, Sherratt, Palmer, Allen, Bloor, A. Waddington (Man...
Front row, L to R: Dobing, Vernon, McIlroy, Viollet, Matthews, Burrows, Skeels

Girls from Langdon Hall College chant "We Want Stoke" and challenge Eric Skeels (left) and Bill Asprey (centre, signing ball) to a game of football on the pavement outside a Manchester Hotel on 5th February 1964 as the Potters prepare to take on Manchester City in the second leg of the League Cup semi-final. The Potters had won the first leg 2-0 at the Victoria Ground thanks to goals from John Ritchie and Bill Asprey, and hung on to a single goal defeat at Maine Road to reach the first major final in Stoke's 100-year history.

League Cup Final

LEICESTER SNATCH THE LEAGUE CUP FROM BRAVE STOKE

By PETER INGALL: Leicester 3, Stoke 2

LEICESTER CITY last night became the third Midland club to win the League Cup—on a 4–3 aggregate—and both teams were cheered to the echo after this Filbert-street thriller.

The man that Leicester had to thank for this success was goalkeeper Gordon Banks, who produced his best England form.

He brought off three fantastic saves from centre forward John Ritchie.

Leicester took a deserved lead in the sixth minute when left winger Mike Stringfellow bamboozled his way past two defenders to score a fine goal.

Inspired by skipper Palmer and the clever promptings of inside left Jimmy McIlroy, Stoke stormed back.

And three minutes after the interval, inside right Dennis Viollet got a clever equaliser.

Then Palmer was carried off the field with an ankle injury.

He returned fifteen minutes later to see inside right David Gibson give Leicester the lead.

Leicester made certain when outside right Howard Riley scored the third goal, but still Stoke hit back.

With seconds to go, the limping Palmer put over a centre for centre half George Kinnell to side-foot the ball home

Keith Bebbington strikes to put Stoke 1-0 up in the first leg of the 1964 League Cup final at the Victoria Ground.

Gordon Banks formed a one-man wall that prevented Stoke taking a lead back to Filbert Street. He's saving here from Ritchie and, below, from Kinnell.

In its early years the League Cup had a two-legged final. Stoke took on Leicester City in the final of just the fourth season of the competition's history, drawing the first leg at the Victoria Ground 1-1 on 15th April 1964. It wasn't a highly regarded competition and only 22,369 attended the first leg of the final.

The Potters had just avoided relegation with four games to go in the League, but had made good Cup progress, defeating Scunthorpe, Bolton, Bournemouth and Rotherham before seeing off Manchester City in the semi-final. John Ritchie had scored two goals in a match on four occasions as Stoke progressed in the competition.

Leicester might have boasted England keeper Gordon Banks in goal, but they were without key defenders Maurice Norman and Frank McLintock in the first leg. Stoke couldn't take advantage, though. They played the better, but struggled to score. Dobing hit the post, Ritchie's shot was saved by Banks and Sjoberg kneed Ritchie's shot off the line. Kinnell lashed in two 30-yarders, which nearly knocked Banks into the net, but the England keeper still kept them out.

Finally, on 62 minutes, winger Keith Bebbington lashed home off the underside of the bar after Banks had parried Asprey's 30-yard drive.

But then disaster struck as inside-left Dave Gibson equalized on 79 minutes when Skeels' clearance hit Heath on the back and fell perfectly for Gibson to guide it home past Leslie. The goal swung the tie and Leicester finished the stronger and with the momentum in their favour.

A week later at Filbert Street there was drama, heroics, excitement and thrills aplenty in a classic tie. Early on Stringfellow pounced to drive past Stoke keeper Bobby Irvine to put Leicester ahead in the tie for the first time, but directly after half-time McIlroy's magnificent crossfield ball found Viollet, who shook off a challenge and left Banks helpless. It was 2-2 on aggregate and all to play for.

Then came a problem for Stoke when inspirational captain Calvin Palmer was injured in a tackle and stretchered off for treatment, before returning 15 minutes later. There were no substitutes allowed at the time and Leicester used their numerical advantage to regain the lead, as Gibson headed into the roof of the net on 69 minutes.

Leicester appeared to clinch the tie when, on 83 minutes, Riley's low shot gave Leicester a 4-2 lead, but in the 89th minute Palmer cut back for Kinnell to score. It was 4-3 and there was still time for Banks to produce a "save in a million" to deny Ritchie's blockbuster in injury time.

It was so near and yet so far for Stoke, who still sought a first major trophy in the club's history.

Stan Hits 50

Stan Matthews gets the rhythm going with Pat Wayne and the Beachcombers, pre-match entertainment before a Stoke home game. Even in his 50th year and not often in the first team reckoning, Stan was a huge pull for a photocall.

Stan blows out the candles on his 50th birthday cake. He actually had an early birthday – over a month before the actual date of 1st February 1965 – due to Stoke's heavy fixture list over the Christmas and New Year period.

Stan announced his retirement in February 1965, but not until he had played his final game for Stoke, in the First Division against Fulham at the Victoria Ground aged 50 years and five days. This makes him the oldest ever top-flight player and the man with the longest footballing career, as his last match came 32 years and 324 days after his debut at Bury. Here he walks out to face the waiting media.

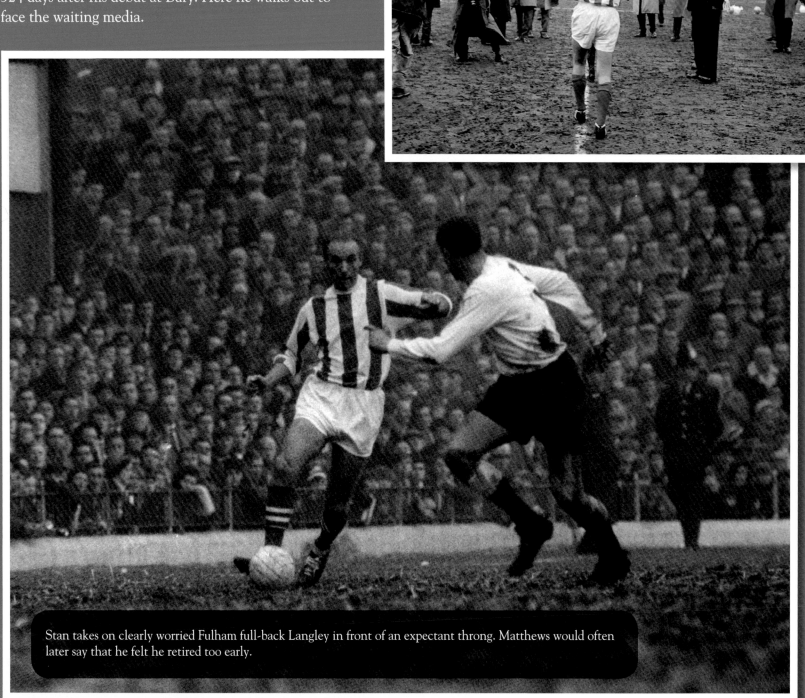

Stan takes on clearly worried Fulham full-back Langley in front of an expectant throng. Matthews would often later say that he felt he retired too early.

Farewell to a Legend

Among many other plaudits Matthews was the first Footballer of the Year, the first European Footballer of the Year and crowned "King of Soccer" in Ghana. To Stoke fans he was always "Our Stan".

Stanley Matthews became football's first knight when he was recognized for his services to football by the Queen in February 1965. Here he arrives at Downing Street for a reception after receiving his award.

Stan proudly poses with a terracotta bust of himself, made by Wedgwood pottery worker Milan Bozic, at a luncheon at Trentham Gardens given by sports writers in honour of the great winger's retirement.

A special farewell match featuring a World All-Stars XI versus a Stan Matthews XI made up of great British players took place at the Victoria Ground on 28th April 1965. Attended by over 34,000 fans and watched on live television by a global audience of 112 million, it was a fabulous occasion on which fans could say goodbye to one of the greatest legends ever to grace a football field. Here Stan welcomes (from left) Alfredo Di Stéfano, Ferenc Puskás and Ladislav Kubala, three legends of the game who came to help the world celebrate the end of Matthews' career.

Stan hangs up his boots.

Matthews is chaired from the field by a host of global football greats and waves a fond farewell. His like will never be seen again.

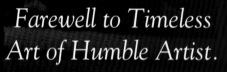

> "Farewell to Timeless Art of Humble Artist.
>
> The Times"

–LEGENDS–

Harry Burrows

On transfer deadline day in March 1965 Tony Waddington signed Aston Villa left-winger Harry Burrows for a knockdown price of £27,000. It was a fantastic 24th birthday present for the nippy flank player who had dynamite in his left boot, and it wasn't long before Burrows got an even better reward when, following a series of blockbuster performances in his first 11 games, Waddo ripped up his contract and awarded him another one with a £5-a-week pay rise!

Harry's nickname was "Cannonball", and justifiably so as he could crack a shot as hard as anyone. He twice finished as City's joint top scorer in the League, matching Dobing's 15 goals in 1967/68 and Ritchie's 14 in 1969/70. He scored when Stoke won a friendly in Barcelona 3-2 in 1969 and netted a hat-trick against his former club as Stoke thrashed Aston Villa 6-1 in December 1966. At 30, he played in all four FA Cup semi-final games in the early 1970s but developed a bad knee injury and was released on a free transfer in 1973.

Harry Burrows buries one of his classic left-footed thunderbolts. This time it's Ipswich Town who are the victims, in a 3-3 draw in November 1969.

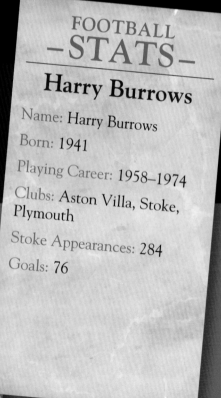

FOOTBALL –STATS–

Harry Burrows

Name: Harry Burrows

Born: 1941

Playing Career: 1958–1974

Clubs: Aston Villa, Stoke, Plymouth

Stoke Appearances: 284

Goals: 76

> " *I'd walk a hundred miles for one of your goals, oh Harry!*
>
> A Boothen End eulogy of left-winger Harry Burrows "

New signing Maurice Setters takes on the gruelling hill run in Trentham Park during pre-season training in 1965.

Stoke goalkeeper Bobby Irvine tries the "Spirometer", a machine which measures lung capacity, as Stoke go scientific in their preparations for the 1965/66 season. Conducting the tests is physical training expert Alan Hargreaves from Madeley Sports College, Staffordshire.

Pre-season Training

Manager Tony Waddington shows the players he can still turn on the style in the gym under the Boothen End.

The Victoria Ground in the mid-1960s.

Stoke Make Their Mark

Goalkeeper John Farmer saves at point blank range from Blackpool's Jimmy Robson, watched by Alan Philpott (third left) and Jimmy Armfield (extreme right). Farmer became an England under-23 international following some sterling performances in Stoke's goal.

The 1967 Stoke squad. Back row (left to right): Maurice Setters, Jackie Marsh, Calvin Palmer, Terry Conroy, Dennis Viollet. Middle row: Bill Bentley, Alan Bloor, Gordon Banks, John Farmer, Eric Skeels, Tony Allen, Frank Mountford (trainer). Front row: John Mahoney, Peter Dobing, Roy Vernon, George Eastham, Harry Burrows, Gerry Bridgwood. Stoke finished 10th in 1966, 12th in 1967 and ninth in 1970 as they earned a reputation as a tough but exciting side.

Inspirational do-or-die skipper Calvin Palmer takes on West Ham full-back Ken Brown. Journalist George Morley once wrote of Palmer: "I can't see management ever being exciting enough for Calvin. He might take up racing to beat Jim Clarke or paratroop into Vietnam." Palmer arrived at Stoke from Nottingham Forest for £30,000 in September 1963 and was the heart and lungs of the team in midfield and then, as his legs began to go, at right-back. He was an abrasive character and fell out with Stoke and then his next club Sunderland in quick succession. He was also a redoubtable fighter and was involved in Stoke's remarkable comeback to win 4-3 at West Ham in November 1967, after being 3-0 down at half-time. It later emerged that Palmer had played on despite hearing that his family had been involved in a car crash earlier that day.

—LEGENDS—

Eric Skeels

Eric Skeels was "Mr Stoke City" for nearly 18 years. He set a club record of 592 for most appearances for the club in competitive games; although Jock McCue played more times for the club, many of his games were during wartime and so are not counted in official statistics. Known by all the players as "Alfie", after his little dog which followed him everywhere, Skeels was a defensive midfielder or centre-half by trade, but filled in across every outfield position in the team during his remarkable and often unheralded career. His greatest attribute was his consistency, although he was also both quick in mind and off the mark. As part of the "Waddington Wall" Skeels won a Second Division championship medal in 1962/63 and a League Cup runner's-up medal in 1964. But he also played his part in the more swashbuckling era of the early 1970s. He only scored seven goals for Stoke, but his first, in August 1962, was a snorter from 30 yards!

FOOTBALL —STATS—

Eric Skeels

Name: Eric Skeels

Born: 1939

Playing Career: 1960–1977

Clubs: Stoke, Port Vale

Stoke Appearances: 592

Goals: 7

LEFT: Stoke City's "Jet Girls", who sold match-day programmes in the mid-1960s. Back Row (left to right) Kathy Ratcliffe (18), Irene Raine (19), Kath Johnson (18). Front Row: Susan Hughes (19), Lynn Bradbury (18), Barbara Merry (19). The programme at that time was called the Ceramic City Clipper (below).

THE CERAMIC CITY CLIPPER

POISE – Terry Conroy streaks away from Manchester City full back Bobby Kennedy during the 1-0 defeat of the champions.
Pictures: JACK BRINDLEY (Stoke City Times)

STOKE CITY FOOTBALL CLUB
OFFICIAL MAGAZINE

Vol. 1. No. 6

PRICE 1/-

ABOVE: Stoke were drawn away at Manchester United in the FA Cup third round in January 1967. The original date was snowed off, so the match was played on a Tuesday evening and a large group of Stoke fans decided to walk overnight all the way to Old Trafford to support their team, on what became known as "The Great Cup Trek".

LEFT: Meanwhile, in contrast, Stoke prepared for the Cup tie by relaxing in their hotel on the outskirts of Manchester. Here manager Tony Waddington talks to former United stars Dennis Viollet and Maurice Setters about returning to defeat their former employers. Stoke lost 0-2.

119

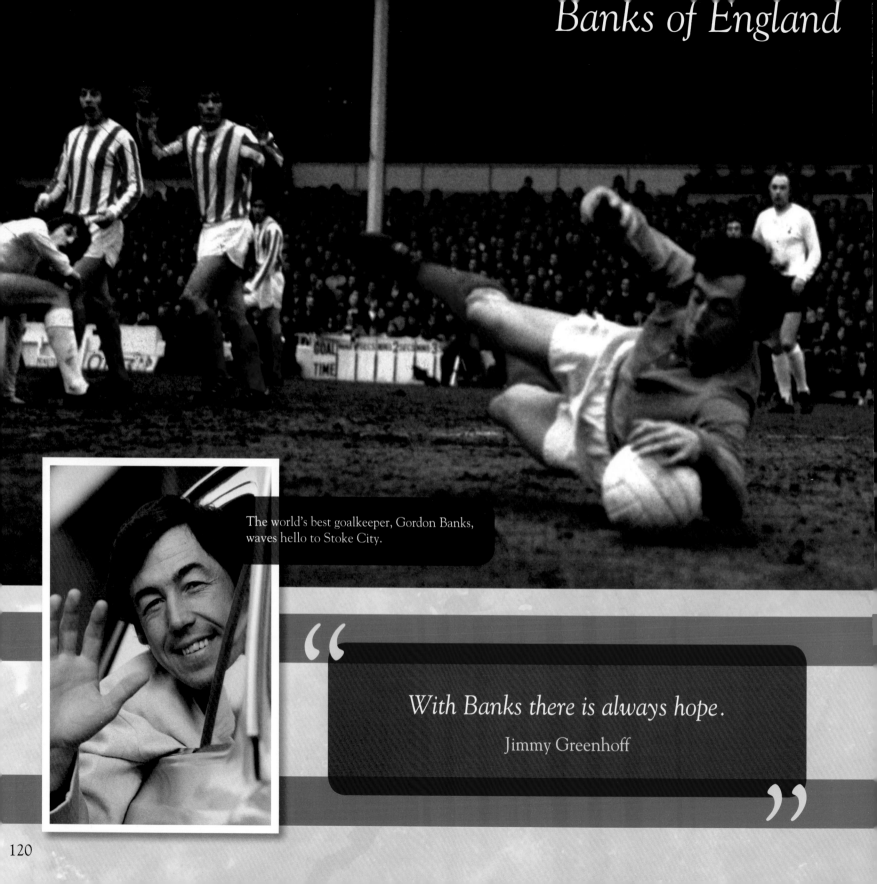

The world's best goalkeeper, Gordon Banks, waves hello to Stoke City.

> " With Banks there is always hope.
>
> Jimmy Greenhoff "

Banks flies through the air to fingertip a shot round the post against Derby County. Banks hardly ever wore gloves, preferring the feel of the ball on his hands.

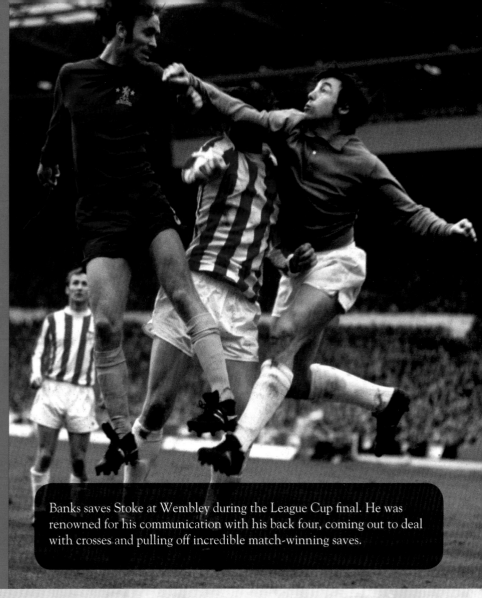

Banks saves Stoke at Wembley during the League Cup final. He was renowned for his communication with his back four, coming out to deal with crosses and pulling off incredible match-winning saves.

Of all Tony Waddington's transfer coups, the arrival of England goalkeeper Gordon Banks truly signalled Stoke City's intent to challenge for major trophies. Banks arrived in April 1967 after being ousted from Leicester by a young talented keeper called Peter Shilton. Waddo spent £52,000 on the world's best custodian and Banks repaid the fee countless times over. One of football's true galaxy of stars in the soccer stratosphere, Banks had starred in England's World Cup triumph less than a year before he moved to the Victoria Ground. On his very first day at Stoke, Banks told his new team-mates in the dressing room that he had come to the club to win things and he produced a period of five years in which his form marked him out quite simply as the greatest goalkeeper of all time. At the height of his powers he made that incredible save from Pelé at the Jalisco Stadium, Guadalajara, at the 1970 World Cup. Banks' heroics earned him an OBE in the Queen's Birthday Honours list and he set a then-record of 73 England caps for a goalkeeper, which included 36 while at Stoke – making Banks City's most capped player. Banks' Stoke career was the story of two semi-final penalties – one mishit by Peter Storey, which went in and denied the Potters a place in the FA Cup final in 1971, the other leathered by Geoff Hurst, which Banks saved and which helped City to reach Wembley the following season. The end of his career would come all too soon after Stoke's first silverware had been won, but Banks remained in the area after he had finished playing and was made president of Stoke City in 2000 after the death of Sir Stanley Matthews.

Four more of Tony Waddington's "Old Crocks", who arrived at Stoke with a reputation and arguably their best years behind them. But Waddo's astute management saw them eke out many more seasons of top-quality performances. Above, George Eastham was a non-playing member of England 1966 World Cup winning squad, and signed for Stoke just after the tournament had finished.

More Old Crocks

Roy Vernon was an experienced Welsh international who arrived in 1965 aged 28. Renowned for skilful play and a short temper, Vernon also had the amazing ability to shower after training without getting a single drop of water on his cigarette!

Scottish left-sided midfielder Willie Stevenson joined Stoke from Liverpool in 1967 at the age of 27 after being ousted from the Reds' line-up by a young Emlyn Hughes.

Peter Dobing joined Stoke from Manchester City for a club record fee of £37,500 after the Potters won promotion to the top flight in 1963 and his own club had been relegated.

One player who was definitely not an "Old Crock" was Welsh midfield dynamo John "Josh" Mahoney. The 20-year-old signed from Crewe in 1967 and took a while to win his place in Stoke's first team, being the substitute in the 1972 League Cup triumph. But when he did break into the side, Mahoney powered across the muddy pitches of the 1970s as an important cog in the centre of midfield alongside Alan Hudson. Tony Waddington called Mahoney a "world-class craftsman" and the big-hearted Welshman displayed the same qualities in playing 51 games for his country.

Pelé's Samba Beat

Stoke's growing reputation for playing good football with big name players paid off with touring foreign sides seeking to play prestige friendlies against the Potters. In September 1969 Pelé's Santos, who were twice world club champions and who arrived at Stoke at the end of a 15-day European tour on a seven-match unbeaten run, won a fantastic game 3-2. The great Brazil striker, Pelé, struck up a friendly rivalry with Gordon Banks, which would come to a climax nine months later in the heat of Guadalajara with Banks' amazing save from a downward header, which was so good the Brazilian was shouting "goal!" but then applauded after the keeper lunged to his right and flicked the bouncing ball up and over the bar.

Santos line-up:

Gilmar
Delgado
Turcão
Lima
Dias
Joel
Maria
Nina
Edu
Pelé
Abel

Denis Smith heads home a corner. The "goal" would have put Stoke 3-1 ahead at half-time as Ritchie and Greenhoff had scored within three minutes, but referee Ken Burns blew for the end of the half a split-second before the ball went in. The controversy raged as the players walked off the pitch and Santos took full advantage in the second half. Edu lashed in from 18-year-old Nina's pass, and then, with seven minutes to go, Pelé produced an incredible moment of magic when, faced with four defenders on the edge of the area, he feinted one way, deftly rolled the ball another, sold all four a dummy and dashed into the space which opened up, before beating Banks with a wicked shot to win the game.

Santos keeper Gilmar punches clear as Stoke pile on the player.

Pelé's vicious left-footed shot flies past Banks to win Santos the game 3-2.

125

Terrace Accident

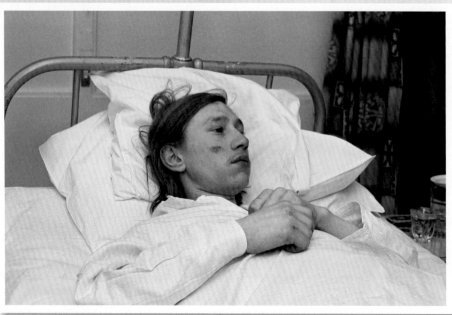

During the game between Stoke and League leaders Leeds on 31st January 1970, a crush barrier on the Boothen End buckled under the pressure of the crowd, causing a collapse. Supporters crushed each other in scenes scarily similar to those at Burden Park 24 years earlier and Hillsborough 19 years later. Over 60 were injured and several were hospitalized, including 20-year-old John Ellis from Leeds (pictured). Above, a policeman stands guard at the scene of the accident, which witnesses amongst the 36,506 crowd said was caused by deliberate "terrifying pushing from behind". A full inquiry was ordered by the chief constable of Staffordshire Mr A Rees. The match ended 1-1.

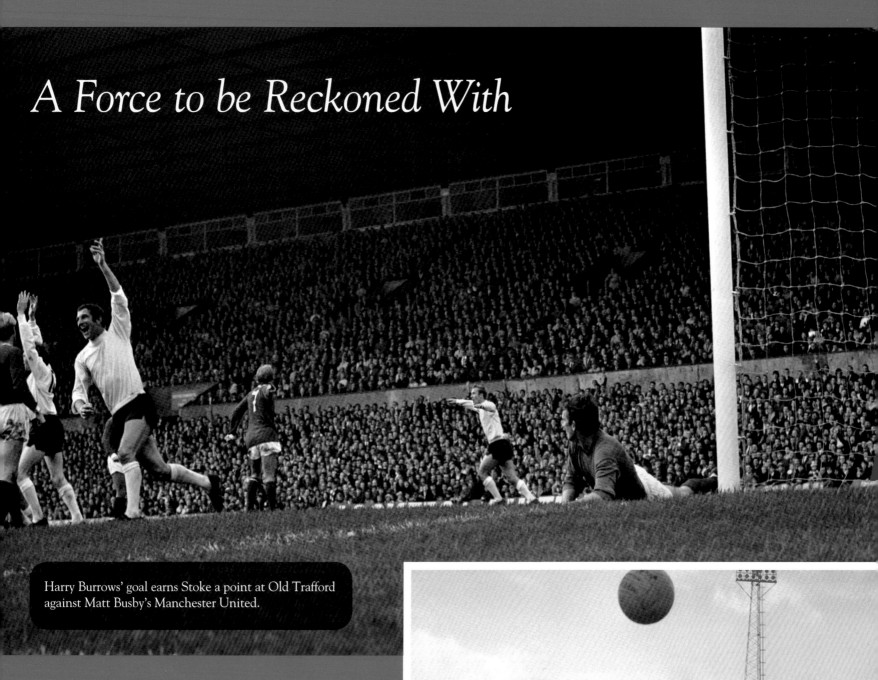

A Force to be Reckoned With

Harry Burrows' goal earns Stoke a point at Old Trafford against Matt Busby's Manchester United.

By the start of the 1970s Stoke City under Tony Waddington had assembled a great squad, with bundles of experience and plenty of talent. It was the start of a golden era for the club.

George Eastham produces a spectacular overhead in the 3-3 home draw with Bobby Robson's Ipswich Town.

Land of Smoke and Glory
1970-75

From left, Jackie Marsh, Josh Mahoney, George Eastham, John Ritchie, Gordon Banks, Jimmy Greenhoff and Mike Pejic celebrate Stoke's first major trophy, the League Cup, on 4th March 1972.

"
Land of Smoke and Glory. Home of Stoke City.
Higher, Higher and Higher. On to Victory.

Boothen End chant in the 1960s and 70s
"

1970 Stoke thrash Arsenal 5-0 at the Victoria Ground. **1971** Arsenal gain revenge by defeating Stoke in the club's first FA Cup semi-final for 72 years, in a replay after the first game ends controversially. Tony Waddington persuades George Eastham to return to the club from South Africa after the FA declare a crackdown on the "tackle from behind". Gordon Banks produces an incredible save from Geoff Hurst's penalty to take the League Cup semi-final to a replay after two legs. **1972** Stoke finally beat West Ham 3-2 in a second replay to reach a major final at Wembley for the very first time. Denis Smith damages his back and appears to be out of contention to play Manchester United in a Cup replay but unricks his spine when getting out of his car and scores. Stoke win 2-1. George Eastham scores the winning goal to add to Terry Conroy's opener as Stoke lift the League Cup. Arsenal dash Stoke's hopes of being the first team to reach both Cup finals in the same season by winning another semi-final replay 2-1. Gordon Banks is voted "Footballer of the Year". Tony Waddington signs another World Cup winner – hat-trick hero Geoff Hurst. Stoke play in Europe for the first time, beating Kaiserslautern 3-1 at home, but losing 4-0 away to go out of the UEFA Cup 5-3 in the first round. Banks loses the sight in one eye after crashing his car on the way home from a physio session at the Victoria Ground. **1973** Alan Hudson signs for Stoke from Chelsea for a club record fee of £240,000. **1974** Stoke take League leaders Leeds' unbeaten record, coming from 2-0 down to win 3-2. John Ritchie's career is ended by having his leg broken in a tackle by Kevin Beattie. Stoke go out of the UEFA Cup to Ajax, but only on away goals. **1975** Terry Conroy's brace in a 2-0 win over Liverpool puts Stoke top of the League with only three games remaining. Stoke miss out on lifting the League title by failing to score in their last three matches, when three wins would have won them the championship.

From left, Jimmy Greenhoff, Mike Bernard, Josh Mahoney, Alan Bloor and Eric Skeels pass the time before the biggest game in the club's history –

–LEGENDS–

John Ritchie

John Ritchie holds the distinction of having scored more competitive goals for Stoke than anyone else. Signed by Tony Waddington from non-League Kettering in 1961, Ritchie grabbed his chance in the 1963/64 season with a scoring streak of nine consecutive games, notching 14 goals. He totalled 18 goals in 29 league games and set a record for the formative League Cup of 10 goals in the season, which has only been beaten by Rodney Marsh and Clive Allen since. One of a dying breed of big, direct and fast centre-forwards, he scored four goals in a league game for Stoke twice, but, having notched 30 and 29 goals respectively in his first full seasons in the side, Ritchie was surprisingly sold to Sheffield Wednesday for £80,000, a new club record for an outgoing transfer fee. Ritchie's departure shocked Stoke fans and Waddington later admitted it was a mistake.

In the summer of 1969 new Wednesday boss Danny Williams decided that Ritchie was past his best and Waddington took the opportunity to rectify his error. Ritchie's return coincided with the arrival of Jimmy Greenhoff's arrival and the pair struck up a telepathic partnership, which one match report famously described thus: "You could have fired a cannonball at Ritchie and he would have nodded it down to Greenhoff's feet." Their partnership was the focal point of Stoke's style of flowing football, which graced the First Division in the early 1970s.

Increasingly injury-prone in his 30s, Ritchie had his leg broken by a heavy Kevin Beattie challenge in September 1974. The complex double fracture ended his career and arguably cost Stoke their chance to win the League. Ritchie's injury came when he was five short of Freddie Steele's club record for League goals, although Big John did improve Steele's overall goalscoring record, which had stood since 1949 at 176.

After retiring Ritchie ran a successful family Pottery firm until his death on 23rd February 2007. A bust of him, depicting his famous two-arm-raised celebration after the FA Cup semi-final of 1971, stands outside the Boothen End of the new Britannia Stadium – a fitting tribute to a true Stoke great.

Fearsome Strikeforce

Ritchie lashes home his second of the game during Stoke's 5-0 humiliation of eventual double winners Arsenal at the Victoria Ground in September 1970.

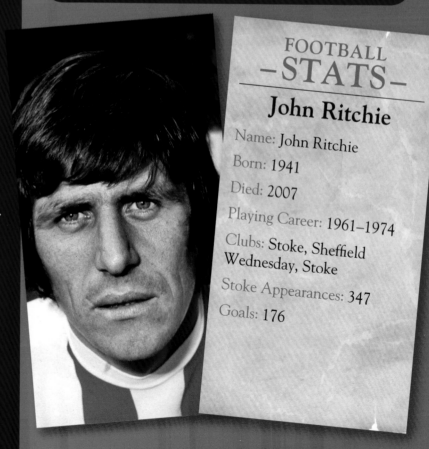

FOOTBALL –STATS–

John Ritchie

Name: John Ritchie

Born: 1941

Died: 2007

Playing Career: 1961–1974

Clubs: Stoke, Sheffield Wednesday, Stoke

Stoke Appearances: 347

Goals: 176

–LEGENDS–

Jimmy Greenhoff

Tony Waddington signed Jimmy Greenhoff from Birmingham City for a club record £100,000 to partner John Ritchie; Greenhoff brought a new dimension to Stoke's play with his passing and movement. He was the perfect foil for Ritchie, feeding off the big striker's knockdowns and spreading the ball wide to Stoke's wing players Terry Conroy, Peter Dobing or, latterly, Sean Haslegrave, Jimmy Robertson and Geoff Salmons.

Greenhoff was also one of the best volleyers of a ball of his, and arguably any other, generation, and he loved Stoke's off-the-cuff style of play. "All I wanted to do was entertain the wonderful fans," he said. "They were a big part of my game, the supporters. So warm – they were different class." The supporters loved him. In February 1971 Greenhoff scored the only goal as Stoke defeated Huddersfield in a close-fought second replay of an FA Cup fourth-round tie at Old Trafford. In an act that set the tone for Stoke fans' deification of Greenhoff, before the next home game an adoring fan ran on to the pitch, knelt and kissed the spot on Greenhoff's right boot that smote the winner. That same right boot would lash a volley towards the Chelsea goal at Wembley a year later which Peter Bonetti found too hot to hold; George Eastham mopped up the rebound to net the winning goal in the League Cup final.

Greenhoff dovetailed beautifully with Alan Hudson after the midfielder's arrival in 1973, but mysteriously the blond-haired forward never won an England cap. He was selected for the England squad a couple of times but was forced to withdraw because Stoke had rearranged League games. England's loss was Stoke's gain as Greenhoff played a major part in the title challenge of 1974/75, which saw Stoke come close to winning the League championship for the first time in their history. He also scored both goals as Stoke lifted the pre-season competition, the Watney Cup, defeating Hull City 2-0 in the final in August 1973.

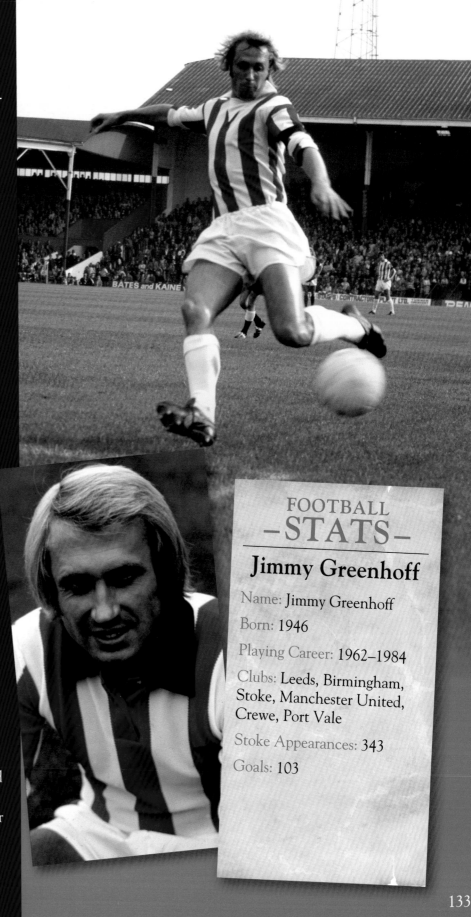

FOOTBALL –STATS–

Jimmy Greenhoff

Name: Jimmy Greenhoff

Born: 1946

Playing Career: 1962–1984

Clubs: Leeds, Birmingham, Stoke, Manchester United, Crewe, Port Vale

Stoke Appearances: 343

Goals: 103

–LEGENDS–

Denis Smith

Standing 5ft 11in tall and with 12st of solid muscle, Denis Smith, a voracious tackler, had a reputation as a hard man who would run through a brick wall for Stoke City. Quite literally he would launch himself at opponents, determined to win the ball or stop his man getting past him at all costs. His no-nonsense approach soon earned him an enormous reputation. When Geoff Hurst joined Stoke from West Ham he declared he only signed so he didn't have to play against Smith and take penalties against Gordon Banks. Alongside his centre-half partner Alan Bloor, Smith formed a fearsome blockade to opposing strikers.

Smith's commitment led to him being idolized by the Stoke fans who would unsettle opposing forwards by singing 'Denis is gonna get you!', although his combative style meant that he ceaselessly nursed one injury or another. Smith broke his leg five times during his career, along with countless other body parts, and constantly sported cuts and grazes. His horrendous injury list left him claiming an entry in the Guinness Book of Records as the most injured man in football. Smith once arrived at the Victoria Ground injured, having not been able to straighten his back all day, but managed to slip something back into place in getting out of his car as his wife dropped him off and was persuaded to play by Tony Waddington after popping into the dressing room to wish his team-mates good luck. He then scored the equalizing goal as Stoke came from behind to defeat Manchester United 2-1 in an FA Cup quarter-final replay in front of 49,000 fans.

Upon leaving Stoke in 1983, Smith won the Fourth Division title with a record 101 points as manager of York City before joining Sunderland in June 1987. He led them out to the Third Division title in his first season and into the First Division in his third. He also managed Bristol City, Oxford United, West Brom and Wrexham in a career that saw him join the elite club of managers to have taken charge of over 1,000 professional games.

The Local Back Four

RIGHT: Denis Smith clatters into Crystal Palace goalkeeper John Jackson in typical buccaneering fashion in 1970.

FOOTBALL
–STATS–

Denis Smith

Name: Denis Smith

Born: 147

Playing Career: 1968–1984

Clubs: Stoke, York

Stoke Appearances: 488

Goals: 42

Alan Bloor tackles Arsenal's George Graham in August 1971.

Alan Bloor partnered Denis Smith at the centre of Stoke's homegrown defence. He had captained England Youth in the early 1960s and broke into Stoke's first team in 1965. At 6ft 1in tall and 13st, Bloor was physically intimidating but a quiet personality.

Consistent and able to read situations and snuff them out before they became dangerous, Bloor and Smith played together 189 times as mainstays of Stoke's exciting, rugged and difficult-to-beat side of the 1970s. Bloor became a carpet salesman in his native Longton, giving rise to the bizarre chant of *"Alan Bloor's Carpet Factory"*, which would occasionally be heard from the Boothen End.

Left-back Mike Pejic was just as teak-tough as Bloor and Smith. The son of an immigrant farmer, Pejic grew up playing as a winger but was converted to left-back by Tony Waddington. Compactly built at 5ft 8in tall "Pej" was a fierce tackler who was no stranger to FA disciplinary proceedings. He was also a fitness fanatic who didn't join in the hectic socializing in which many of Stoke's players indulged during the 1970s. He won three England caps in 1974 under caretaker-manager Joe Mercer but was not given a chance under Don Revie's reign. Sold to Everton for £135,000, he moved on to Aston Villa before retiring to become a coach at Port Vale, manager at Chester and later academy director at Stoke, Plymouth and Ipswich.

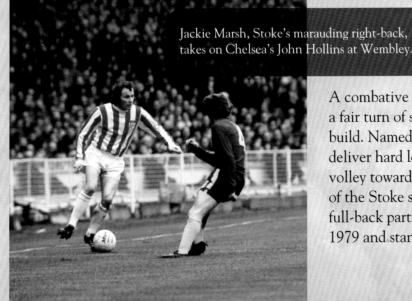

Jackie Marsh, Stoke's marauding right-back, takes on Chelsea's John Hollins at Wembley.

A combative right-back, Jackie Marsh also was blessed with good control and a fair turn of speed for a small chunky player, who did not have an athletic build. Named "Jo" by his team mates, he specialized in bombing forward to deliver hard low crosses on the run, which allowed forwards to flick on or volley towards goal. Unlike Pejic, Marsh liked to socialize, along with many of the Stoke squad, but Jackie did share a relish for a hard tackle with his full-back partner. Having made his debut in 1967, Marsh kept his place until 1979 and stands eighth in the all-time appearance list for Stoke.

FA Cup Dreams Shattered

Stoke's dynamic and tigerish team battled through seven matches to reach the FA Cup semi-final for the first time for 72 years and only the second time in their history, thanks to a 3-2 comeback victory over Hull in the quarter-finals.

27th March 1971

In the semi-final at Hillsborough, Stoke played brilliantly in the first half and went into a two-goal lead after Smith blocked a clearance and the ball rebounded into the net, and then Ritchie latched onto Charlie George's awful back pass to round Wilson and score (below), much to his and all the Stoke fans' delight. Stoke were so much better than Arsenal that talk was of how many the team would score in winning through to Wembley.

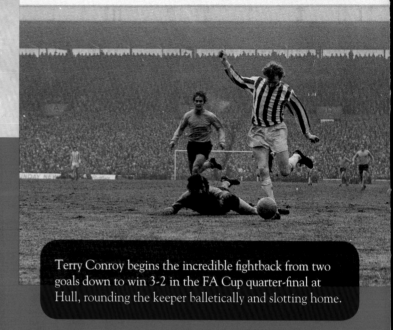

Terry Conroy begins the incredible fightback from two goals down to win 3-2 in the FA Cup quarter-final at Hull, rounding the keeper balletically and slotting home.

But the fairytale was not to be. First Arsenal midfielder Peter Storey scored from 18 yards with a deflected shot early in the second half, and then, with the four minutes of injury time indicated by the referee up, Arsenal were awarded a controversial free-kick, which looked as if it was more of a foul on Pejic than a foul by Pejic. The set piece was cleared for a corner after a mad scramble, but from the flag-kick Frank McLintock headed goalwards and, with Banks beaten, Mahoney dived to his right to tip the ball round the post. Stoke were stunned by this chain of events and Storey's badly hit penalty beat Banks, who was left wrong-footed. A trip to Wembley had been denied in the cruellest of circumstances and Arsenal won the replay comfortably.

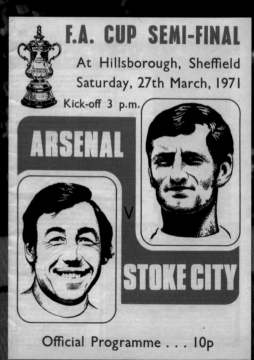

F.A. CUP SEMI-FINAL

At Hillsborough, Sheffield
Saturday, 27th March, 1971

Kick-off 3 p.m.

ARSENAL

v

STOKE CITY

Official Programme . . . 10p

LEFT: Stoke fans on the Kop at Hillsborough in fine fettle as the team lead 2-0 at half-time. The second half would give rise to far different emotions.

Stoke's nemesis, Peter Storey, scorer of both Arsenal goals in their remarkable comeback, is tackled by Mike Bernard.

McLintock's header is arrowing into the corner of Stoke's goal and John Mahoney (second left) is about to throw himself to his right and touch it round the post with his fingertips. The ensuing penalty was scored by Storey and Arsenal won the replay as a deflated Potters' side had the stuffing knocked out of them.

Bob Wilson saves as Stoke mount a rare attack in the 1971 FA Cup semi-final replay at Villa Park, which Arsenal won 2-0.

" Walking out of the ground was like walking to the gallows.

Stoke fan reliving the horrendous aftermath of the Cup semi-final draw at Hillsborough "

More Semi-final Drama!

Gordon Banks reaches up his left hand to tip Geoff Hurst's late blockbuster penalty over the bar to keep Stoke level at 2-2 in the 1972 League Cup semi-final and force a replay. Hurst had not missed a spot-kick for four years and had scored one in the first leg at Stoke, but the tension of the penalty was such that Bobby Moore crouched, head in hands (see inset opposite), in his own half not wanting to look. After this stunning and vital save the Stoke defenders were so elated they almost forgot to defend the ensuing corner until Banks marshalled them. The save has gone down in Stoke folklore. Banks, already moving to his right, arched back to fist the ball over the bar when it seemed as if Hurst's bullet down the centre had beaten him. It was conservatively estimated that that save put £100,000 into Stoke's coffers, with replay, Wembley and subsequent European competitions.

Mike Bernard pokes the ball over the line during the Old Trafford mudbath that was the second and deciding replay of the 1972 League Cup semi-final between Stoke and West Ham. Strangely, the beaten goalkeeper is Bobby Moore, as regular keeper Bobby Ferguson was off the pitch for treatment.

From right, Jimmy Greenhoff, Jackie Marsh and cigar-smoking Mike Bernard celebrate reaching the club's first ever major final.

26ᵗʰ January 1972

The League Cup semi-final between Stoke and West Ham developed into a saga lasting four matches, 390 minutes and 49 days from start to climactic finish. The second replay at Old Trafford was action-packed, controversial and took place amidst a torrential downpour. First, Hammers keeper Ferguson was injured diving at Terry Conroy's feet and Bobby Moore went in goal. McDowell gave away a penalty and Mike Bernard stepped up to take the spot-kick, but hit it straight at Moore. England's captain could not hold on, though, and Bernard lashed in the rebound. West Ham went in front thanks to two long-range goals, but Stoke hit back to level just before half-time, when Dobing cracked home from 25 yards.

This monumental tie was settled when a loose ball fell to impish Irishman Terry Conroy 20 yards from goal. Conroy hit a searing volley, which rocketed into the corner of the returned but dazed Ferguson's net. Stoke had won through to a Wembley final at last!

Getting Ready for the Big Day!

Stoke-on-Trent had never seen anything like the kind of Cup fever that engulfed it during February 1972: shop windows were dressed, good-luck messages hung out of windows and off bridges, and huge celebratory cakes were baked and decorated. The Potters were finally going to Wembley!

Some made waiting more comfortable than others!

The players record Stoke's Cup final song 'We'll Be With You!', written by Tony Hatch and Jackie Trent, a Potteries-born songwriting partnership perhaps most famous for penning the theme tune to the Australian TV soap opera *Neighbours*.

Fans queue as far as the eye can see down the side of the main stand at the Victoria Ground to buy their Cup final tickets.

The squad pose in their Cup final suits. Terry Conroy appears to have missed the instruction to wear shorts!

'We'll Be With You!' reached number 35 in the charts as Stoke triumphed at Wembley, and is still played as the teams walk out before games at the Britannia Stadium well into the 21st century.

Eastham, Ritchie, Dobing, Mahoney and Banks kill some time by larking around for a photographer at the club's pre-final bolt-hole of the Selsdon Park Hotel, Surrey.

Gordon Banks accepts a gift of a bunch of flowers from the Chelsea squad. Many of the outfield players received desktop cigarette lighters. Were the Blues trying to put Stoke off?!

The Stoke players' wives and girlfriends prepare for the journey down to Wembley. From left: Mrs Stevenson, Mrs Ritchie, Miss Brooks (Terry Conroy's partner), Mrs Bloor, Mrs Greenhoff, Mrs Smith, Miss Johnson (Jackie Marsh's partner), Mrs Eastham, Mrs Pejic, Mrs Skeels, Mrs Bernard, Mrs Banks.

Jeff Hand and Valerie Podmore were so desperate to see the final that they moved their wedding from 4th March (the day of the final) to the previous day. Here they proudly show off their Cup final tickets on the eve of their nuptials.

Stoke fans take over Wembley for their first big day out in 109 years of history.

Terry Conroy nods in the opening goal after just five minutes. The winger was so stunned by seeing his name go up on the Wembley scoreboard at either end of the ground that he played the next 10 minutes or so in a complete daze.

George Eastham cracks home a rebound after Peter Bonetti had turned aside Jimmy Greenhoff's thunderbolt volley. The goal put Stoke 2-1 ahead, following Peter Osgood's equalizing goal just before half-time. Eastham remains the oldest man to score a winning goal in a Cup final at Wembley; he was aged 35 years and 161 days.

Stoke defender Jackie Marsh lost one of his contact lenses during the latter stages of the final, meaning he couldn't see! Here he can be seen eyeing the errant lens, which he'd found on the Wembley turf, before putting it back into his eye to see out the game.

One Stoke player had a double celebration to toast as midfielder Mike Bernard's wife gave birth to a beautiful baby daughter, Kimberley, on the day of the final.

Gordon Banks plunges at the feet of Chris Garland deep into added time as Chelsea desperately seek an equalizer. Banks was saving the blushes of Mike Bernard, whose weak back pass had left Garland clean through on goal. It was a hearts in mouths moment, but Banks of England saved the day and Stoke clung on to win.

Gordon Banks enjoys Stoke's moment of triumph.

The Cup Comes Home

An incredible reception awaited Stoke's players and staff as they alighted from the train at Barlaston in the south of the city and paraded the Cup through the streets atop an open bus.

Goalscorer Terry Conroy allows a young fan a hold of Stoke's cherished Cup on the train on the way back from London.

Captain Peter Dobing shows off the League Cup.

A huge welcome awaits from young supporters who have climbed on top of the library.

The official reception stage outside the King's Hall, Stoke – fans partied long and hard into the night.

The emotion of the occasion gets too much for this fan.

George Eastham relaxes at Selsdon Park in the days leading up to the League Cup final.

Eastham's wife Wendy gives the winning goalscorer a Cup final kiss.

Eastham shows Argentinian wonderkid Carlos Babington around the Victoria Ground in January 1972. Waddington wanted to sign the 22-year-old superstar from Atlético Huracán, but Babington, known as El Ingles (the Englishman) in his home country due to having British ancestors, chose to stay in Argentina, signing the following year for German club SG Wattenscheid 09. Increasingly, Eastham was being groomed to take over from Waddington, becoming a talent spotter and then coach for Stoke.

–LEGENDS–

George Eastham

George Eastham may have only tapped in an unmissable chance to win the League Cup, but in doing so he wrote his name unforgettably into the annals of Stoke City folklore. It was the culmination of an incredible career as Eastham had initially become famous for being the man to finally break the yoke of serfdom that hung around footballers' necks until 1961, when he took on his employers, Newcastle United, in a court case as he wanted to leave. The "retain and transfer system", which had been in operation until then and that allowed clubs to dictate what players did was smashed as a result and footballers became free to command much larger wages and move at the end of their contracts.

Eastham joined Arsenal and, as a talented and ball-playing inside-forward with a lovely touch and magical left foot, played his way into England's World Cup squad, although he did not make an appearance in the tournament. He signed for Stoke in the summer of 1966 and, despite nearing 30, proved to be one of Waddington's most astute older signings. His calm experience reflected well on the emerging youngsters in the late sixties, such as Terry Conroy, John Mahoney and John Ritchie. At 5ft 7in tall, and just 9½st, Eastham did not relish a physical battle, relying instead on his passing skills to make an impact: he was universally known as "Gentleman George" throughout his career. He played until his 38th year and acted as coach both for Stoke and in South Africa in the summer months, before succeeding Tony Waddington in the manager's seat at the Victoria Ground in 1977. His tenure would prove to be unsuccessful and Eastham was sacked just a year later.

More FA Cup Heartache

> "I couldn't do or say anything. I felt so numb I just sat in the bath for a long, long time."
>
> Gordon Banks

Jimmy Greenhoff's penalty gives Stoke the lead in the FA Cup semi-final replay at Goodison Park. However, a controversial penalty awarded for nothing more than a nudge by Dobing on Armstrong brought Arsenal level. The match was heading towards extra time when another storm engulfed the tie. Incredibly, one of the linesmen mistook a white-coated ice-cream seller on the far side of the ground for one of Stoke's defenders and waved play on when Radford was 10 yards offside. The striker raced clear to net the winning goal, which stood despite Stoke's heated protests to referee Walker. Defeat cost Stoke the chance of becoming the first club to ever reach two Wembley Cup finals in one season.

WEMBLE
WE COM

PENALTY! Goalkeeper

By the time Stoke and Arsenal were drawn together again in a second successive FA Cup semi-final in April 1972, the teams were fierce rivals. Tensions ran high and spilled over into on-field violence, which made the match at Villa Park far less of a spectacle. A tight game was made more dramatic by Gunners keeper Bob Wilson injuring a knee and having to leave the field, being replaced by centre-forward John Radford who proceeded to stop everything Stoke could throw at him and earn his side a replay.

The inquest begins in Arsenal's defence after Peter Simpson's own goal brings Stoke level at 1-1, but despite dominating the second half Stoke couldn't find a way to break through.

GEORGE, RADFORD LAND FINAL KNOCK-OUT

By KEN JONES: Stoke 1, Arsenal 2

Arsenal's turn to be lucky after double penalty drama

GOAL! John Radford hits the seventy-sixth minute winner and Arsenal are back at Wembley.

SO HAPPY FANS SALUTE THREE-GOAL BRIGHTON

By NIGEL CLARKE: Brighton 3, Blackburn 0

Stoke's World Cup Heroes

World Cup-winning hero Gordon Banks takes the accolades after being announced as Footballer of the Year for the 1971/72 season. He was also named as Sportsman of the Year.

In the summer of 1972 England's hat-trick hero from the World Cup triumph, Geoff Hurst, signed for Stoke for £80,000, saying: "I joined Stoke so I wouldn't have to play against Denis Smith or take penalties against Gordon Banks!" Hurst scored 37 goals in 128 games for Stoke before winding down his career with West Brom, whom he joined for £20,000 in 1975.

Hurst shoots for goal in typically powerful style in September 1974, beating the tackle of Derby's David Nish.

Into Europe

Victory in the League Cup final meant Stoke had qualified for Europe for the first time. In the UEFA Cup first round they were drawn with German side Kaiserslautern and won the first leg on 13th September 1972 at the Victoria Ground 3-1. But City were undone in the second leg and lost 0-4, not helped by substitute John Ritchie being sent off within 10 seconds of entering the field after he jostled with Yugoslavian international midfielder Idriz Hošić and lashed out after receiving a sly punch. Stoke went out 3-5 on aggregate.

Geoff Hurst sees his shot saved by Kaiserslautern keeper Josef Elting.

Terry Conroy's shot flies into the Kaiserslautern net to put Stoke 1-0 ahead in their first ever European tie at the Victoria Ground.

Denis Smith goes close to adding a fourth goal.

The ball is in the net for Stoke's second goal in the first-leg UEFA Cup defeat of Kaiserslautern, scored by number nine, John Ritchie.

Geoff Hurst converts Conroy's cross to give Stoke a magnificent first victory in Europe. It wouldn't be such plain sailing in the second leg, however.

FOOTBALL
–STATS–

Terry Conroy

Name: Terry Conroy

Born: 1946

Playing Career: 1967–1981

Clubs: Stoke, Crewe

Stoke Appearances: 271

Goals: 49

Republic of Ireland Appearances: 26

Goals: 2

–LEGENDS–

Terry Conroy

Terry Conroy, Stoke's first ever goalscorer in European competition, was the quintessential cheeky Irish chappy. The life and soul of the party ever since Tony Waddington signed him from Glentoran in 1967, Conroy's exuberance was expressed in his wing play. Comfortable on either flank, or through the middle after Ritchie's retirement, TC, as he became universally known, could find the net too. He stood out for many reasons – skill, energy, drive and commitment, but also his looks: waiflike, almost translucent legs, often with socks rolled down to ankles and no shin pads, and wild, wavy red hair.

In January and February 1971 Conroy was directly responsible for each of Stoke's eight goals, scoring five, making two for Greenhoff and having a shot deflected in by a defender who was credited with an own goal. The ability to make something out of nothing endeared him to the Stoke faithful who sang his praises *"Terry, Terry Conroy, Terry Conroy on the wing!"* His best goal came in the 5-0 thrashing of Arsenal in September 1970 when he lashed in a first-time rocket from 30 yards, which finished third in *Match of the Day*'s Goal of the Season competition; he celebrated in distinctive style, running behind the goal with both arms raised aloft.

Not only did Terry Conroy score the opening goal in the 1972 League Cup final, but it was his cross that created the havoc that led to Eastham netting the winning goal.

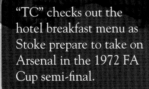

"TC" checks out the hotel breakfast menu as Stoke prepare to take on Arsenal in the 1972 FA Cup semi-final.

> *The ball bounced up, I just put my head on it and the next thing I knew there was this noise and I saw the ball in the back of the net – I'd scored!*
>
> Terry Conroy, scorer of Stoke's first goal in the League Cup final at Wembley in 1972

21st October 1972. Gordon Banks harangues referee Roger Kirkpatrick, who had given a controversial free-kick to Liverpool as Banks had taken too many steps with the ball. The free-kick had resulted in a last-minute winning goal for the Reds.

The following day Banks was still preoccupied with the injustices of Anfield and, driving home from a physiotherapy session at the Victoria Ground, he crashed his Ford Granada when he tried to overtake a crawling lorry, and swerved off the road to avoid an oncoming Austin A60 van. The windscreen smashed into his face and damaged his eyes.

The crash made headline news and news flashes interrupted programmes to inform a shocked nation of Banks' plight. It soon emerged that, after hours of delicate operations and days of recuperation, his right eye was badly and irreparably lacerated. It was a terrible and premature end to a great career, and a huge loss to the world of football. Thousands of well-wishers from across the globe sent Gordon cards and presents in the hope that he might get better.

Disaster for Banks

The dark glasses hide some of the damage to Stoke and England goalkeeper Gordon Banks' eyes.

A happy scene as Gordon Banks runs out to play his first game following his accident, but, alas, it was only a local friendly and the keeper would soon realize that the loss of sight in his right eye was far too severe to be overcome well enough to play at the very top level again. Despite various comeback attempts Banks was forced to call time on his top-flight career.

The season after the crash, when Stoke played at Anfield, Liverpool manager Bill Shankly invited Banks to walk around the ground with him before the game kicked off. The world's finest goalkeeper was greeted to a warm and prolonged Kop welcome – a show of appreciation of all that he had done for England. Here, Banks returns the compliment, raising Shankly's arm to the Kop by way of acknowledging the Liverpool boss's kindness.

The press conference at which Tony Waddington revealed to the waiting press the extent of Gordon Banks' (foreground on left) injuries.

Stoke already had an experienced replacement for Banks in their ranks – understudy keeper John Farmer, who had made his debut in 1965 as an 18-year-old.

Replacing Gordon

Farmer tips a shot onto the post and away to safety against Leeds in 1973. Farmer rarely let anyone down, but Waddington wanted to replace Banks' dominant persona in the penalty area and so, in November 1974, he plunged into the transfer market once again.

Peter Shilton, signed from Leicester for a world record fee for a goalkeeper of £325,000, is greeted on his first day at the Victoria Ground by newly signed-up Club's sartorial elegance.

Mirror Sport

Friday, November 22, 1974
Telephone: (STD code 01)—353 0246

JIM BEATS LOCK-OUT

Leicester boss dashes to sign Toshack

By CHRIS JAMES

JIMMY BLOOM-FIELD yesterday did more than half a million pounds worth of transfer business—and was then locked out of the Football League HQ.

The Leicester boss sold England goalkeeper Peter Shilton to Stoke for a record £340,000 and then dashed to Lytham St. Annes to sign Welsh star John Toshack from Liverpool in a £200,000 deal.

The record-breaker

All smiles at the Shiltons. Here are £340,000 father Peter, his wife Sue and son Michael after yesterday's record deal.

Climb

SHILTON'S WORTH TEN POINTS

By NIGEL CLARKE

Battler Joey takes title

By HOWARD BOOTH

Platignum Gifts

RACING MIRROR with the BIG dog card Pages 24, 25

England's two greatest goalkeepers in training. The session was a publicity stunt following Shilton's signing, as Banks was by now Stoke's goalkeeping coach.

Shilton saves spectacularly at Arsenal. Despite being one of the greatest goalkeepers ever, Shilton did not gel with the Stoke defence. He was not as vocal as Banks had been and did not come out to sweep up through balls, which led to confusion. His form dropped off and he lost his England place to Ray Clemence. In his autobiography Shilton called his time at Stoke his "lost years". Waddo's gamble had not paid off.

Stoke were often asked to travel abroad and play friendlies. Here they warm up in the Olympic Stadium in Athens prior to taking on Persepolis, a game which ended 1-1.

Huddy Arrives

Hudson was a fashionista and playboy who had grown up on the King's Road in the centre of Chelsea. Here he poses with models Renate (left) and Cindy in typically unabashed style.

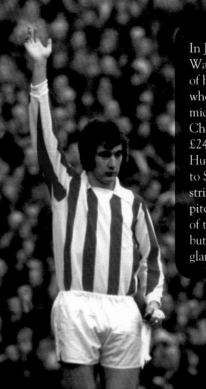

In January 1973 Tony Waddington pulled off one of his biggest transfer coups when he signed creative midfielder Alan Hudson from Chelsea for a club record £240,000. Not only did Hudson add a new dimension to Stoke's play, pulling the strings from the centre of the pitch as Stoke became one of the best teams in the land, but he injected a good deal of glamour into the Potteries.

Alan Hudson walks on water.

Banner in the Boothen End in the mid 1970s

England's newest star takes a well-earned rest after he masterminded the 2-0 victory against West Germany in March 1975.

Hudson crunches into a tackle at Arsenal, proving he could get stuck in as well as perform "the Working Man's Ballet".

FOOTBALL -STATS-

Alan Hudson

Name: Alan Hudson

Born: 1951

Playing Career: 1968–1985

Clubs: Chelsea, Stoke, Arsenal, Chelsea, Stoke

Stoke Appearances: 144

Goals: 9

England Appearances: 2

Goals: 0

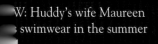

W: Huddy's wife Maureen
 swimwear in the summer
.

-LEGENDS-

Alan Hudson

Alan Hudson swaggered across the muddy Victoria Ground pitch during Stoke's halcyon period of the 1970s. He was a footballing genius and playboy in the 1970s maverick mould, but, in Tony Waddington, Hudson found a man he could admire and who could handle him.

Playboy Hudson soon discovered Stoke's answer to the bright lights of the King's Road, Chelsea – a nightclub in Hanley called The Place, which Stoke's players ritually visited on a Monday night. A heavy drinker, Hudson found a bosom buddy in Geoff Salmons, a £160,000 signing from Sheffield United in the summer of 1974, although most of the Stoke squad were prone to late-night drinking sessions.

Without doubt one of the most gifted players of his generation, Hudson was the catalyst which turned a very good Stoke side into a championship-challenging one for two years in the mid 1970s. By his own admission Hudson played the best football of his career at Stoke as he combined brilliantly with Jimmy Greenhoff. Waddington was moved to call Stoke's style of football the "Working Man's Ballet", a title which Hudson gave to his 1997 autobiography.

> " *You are still the best player in the country by a mile. Ram it down their throats on the pitch.* "
>
> Telegram from George Best to Alan Hudson, 1975

161

Fighting for the Title

Football was very much a man's game in the 1970s. Stoke could play some exceptional stuff, but they could also scrap for their lives. Here Liverpool's Emlyn Hughes and Ray Clemence take exception to a Denis Smith challenge on John Toshack.

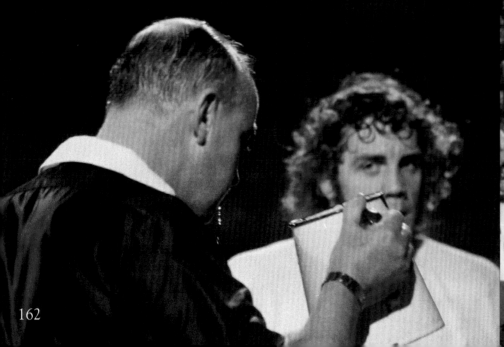

Terry Conroy and Manchester City's Rodney Marsh come to blows in November 1974. John Mahoney is about to wade in and "help".

Mike Pejic falls foul of referee Walker and goes into the book – again.

Denis Smith's elbow introduces itself to Arsenal goalkeeper Bob Wilson's forehead. Little protection was given to goalkeepers at that time. Smith relished clattering into them at every opportunity.

162

Defeating Mighty Leeds

Alan Hudson (foreground, left) watches Jimmy Greenhoff battle it out in midfield with the team known across the country as "Dirty Leeds". Don Revie's side arrived at the Victoria Ground on 23rd February 1974 undefeated after 29 games of the season, looking to set a new record of 30. Leeds went 2-0 ahead in the first half in controversial circumstances but Mike Pejic and Alan Hudson struck to bring Stoke back level at half-time.

The Stoke squad in the summer of 1974 – the middle of this halcyon period in the club's history. Back row (left to right): Kevin Lewis, Alan Dodd, Terry Conroy, Eric Skeels, Sean Haslegrave. Centre row (left to right): Mike Pejic, Denis Smith, John Farmer, Mike McDonald, Alan Bloor, John Mahoney, Jackie Marsh. Front row (left to right): Jimmy Robertson, Alan Hudson, Geoff Hurst, Jimmy Greenhoff, John Ritchie, Geoff Salmons.

Denis Smith heads the winning goal as Stoke recover from a two-goal deficit to win 3-2 and end Leeds' unbeaten run and pursuit of the record which mattered so much to them. This classic match was one of the greatest games ever at the stadium.

Total Football

In the autumn of 1974 Stoke played European giants Ajax in the first round of the UEFA Cup after qualifying by finishing fifth in the First Division in 1973/74. Here Jimmy Greenhoff exchanges pennants with Ajax skipper Ruud Krol. The Dutch club had recently sold Johan Cruyff to Barcelona, but still boasted the likes of Arie Haan, Johnny Rep, Piet Schrijvers and the Mühren brothers in their talented side.

The first leg at the Victoria Ground ended 1-1 after Denis Smith's header equalized Krol's 30-yard thunderbolt.

HARRY MILLER in Enschede says: 'Away goals rule is the cruellest in European football'

IPSWICH TUMBLE TO A DUTCH DOUBLE

Injured keeper defies a Talbot thunderbolt

IPSWICH'S dream of conquering on two fronts, in Britain and Europe, collapsed last night in the face of the cruellest rule in football.

The team who had set their heart, after much soul-searching, on going flat-out for the First Division and the UEFA Cup were beaten because away goals count double in all European competitions.

Yet, at the final unhappy crunch, there was also another personal reason for their exit.

Three minutes from time, Henry Ardesch, a 30-year-old goalkeeper, who played only after a pre-match pain-killing injection for a shoulder injury, produced a better than this cramped Dutch provincial town ground.

Hibs hammer Norwegians

Hibs 9, Rosenborg 1
(Agg.: Hibs win 12—3)

HIBERNIAN ran riot at Easter Road last night.

But the Norwegians shocked the Scots when Iversen scored from a free kick after sixteen minutes. Then Hibs hit three goals in two minutes through Munro and Harper (two).

As the slaughter continued, Munro hit his second. The others came from Stanton (two), Cropley (two penalties) and Gordon.

FC TWENTE 1, IPSWICH 1
(Aggregate 3—3, Twente win on away-goals rule)

He literally somersaulted backwards to turn away a ten-yard thunderbolt from Brian Talbot.

That was the moment Ipswich hearts sank at last of Europe following a weekend of injuries and illness.

It is to Robson's great credit that he decided otherwise. He and coach Cyril Lea were continually on the touchline urging their men forward in a tense and tremendous second half.

Robson said: "I promised we would fight—and we did. The Dutch said they have never seen a side attack like we did.

"But, at the finish, it all came down to that tremendous save from Talbot."

Twente, a side full of bold and brave effort by the young side who have excited the First Division with their attacking football.

Manager Bobby Robson admitted his temptation was to pass quietly out of Europe following a weekend of injuries and illness.

Twente, a side full of flair and imagination, scored first after seven minutes. Rene Notten, an outstanding player, made the run and cross from the left for Jaap Bos to score.

Ipswich were level seven minutes later, with a goal in keeping with their magnificent performance. Colin Harper found Trevor Whymark and he played the ball to Bryan Hamilton who scored with a fierce right-foot volley.

Ipswich pressed as time ran out, but that super save and the sad rule finally proved Ipswich's undoing.

STOKE SCARE AJAX

From JOHN BEAN in Amsterdam: Ajax 0, Stoke 0

(Agg.: 1—1, Ajax win on away goal)

BRAVE Stoke went within an ace of toppling former European champions Ajax here last night.

At the final whistle a hail of seat covers were thrown by angry fans at their former idols who squeezed through this UEFA tie on the double value of their away goal in the Potteries a fortnight ago.

The match had had an explosive start with Mike Pejic and Blankenborg booked for a touchline flare-up, while Geoff Hurst was next to have his name taken for a mere gesture of frustration when he was denied a corner.

Stamped

But Stoke, refusing to be rattled, twice almost snatched a crucial goal from Jimmy Greenhoff with two snap efforts.

Stoke stamped their impressed Olympic Stadium in the second half by powering over high balls to Schrijvers which kept the Dutch 'keeper at full stretch.

Ajax were frankly a flop and as their frustration built up spasms of slow handclapping broke out.

Jim's lecture does the trick

Petrosani 2
Dundee Utd. 0
(Agg.: Dundee Utd. win 3—2)

DESPITE last night's defeat in Rumania, Dundee Utd reached the second round of the Cup Winners Cup.

The three goals they scored in the first leg at Tannadice saw them home, but it was a grim struggle when Petrosani went ahead through Boenal and Tonca.

An interval lecture from manager Jim McLean stiffened the Scots' resistance.

DRAB WATFORD GET THE BIRD

Watford 1, Hereford 1

WATFORD'S bid to record their first double of the season ended with slow handclaps.

The 5,000 fans who saw Watford take a first half lead and then throw away a point.

Stewart Scullion put Watford ahead from the penalty spot in the thirty-third minute after former England international Terry Paine had handled in a goalmouth scramble. In the seventy-ninth minute Hereford equalised through a header by Dixie McNeil.

SEXTON LEARNS FATE TODAY

By JACK STEGGLES

THE future of Chelsea manager Dave Sexton will be announced this afternoon with all the signs pointing to Sexton being sacked after seven years in charge at Stamford Bridge.

Chelsea have slumped sadly in recent weeks and chairman Brian Mears has spent the last couple of days discussing the critical position with the rest of the board.

They have decided on the action needed to halt the slide and will make it public at lunch-time.

Mears was galvanised into action after watching Chelsea jeered from the field after losing at home to Wolves last Saturday.

Chelsea have yet to win at home this season and gates have slumped alarmingly—way below the 35,000 break-even figure needed to pay for the new 22m stand.

LEAGUE MATCHES

Gills skipper is sent off

Blackburn 4, Gillingham 1

GILLINGHAM skipper Joe Jacques was sent off for a foul in the fifty-third minute of a grim night for the Kent club and Dave Galvin and Keith Lindsay were also booked.

Blackburn's Don Martin ignored all the incidents to help himself to a 22-minute hat-trick after Damian Richardson had put Gillingham ahead in seven minutes. Pal Hilton made it 4—1.

Aldershot 3, Halifax 1

INJURY-HIT Aldershot romped to their first win in seven matches to pull away from the Third Division danger zone.

Defender Richard Walden put them on the victory trail in the eleventh minute. Halifax hit back through Alan Jones, but goals from Jack Howarth and Terry Bell sealed Aldershot's victory.

Peterboro' 1, Southend 0

SOUTHEND'S promotion challenge received a set-back against a determined injury-hit Peterborough side.

The visitors had four men booked, Chris Guthrie, Dave Cunningham and Neil Townsend. The goal that beat them was a superb individual effort from David Gregory.

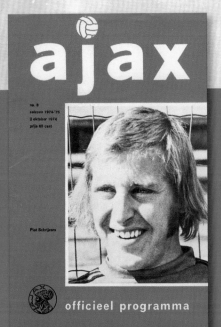

ajax

no. 8
seizoen 1974-75
2 oktober 1974
prijs 60 cent

Piet Schrijvers

officieel programma

The programme from the second leg of the tie at Amsterdam's Olympic Stadium.

Stoke only lost to Ajax on away goals, after the second leg ended goalless, and would have knocked the Dutch club out had Jimmy Robertson put this chance into the net rather than over the bar via Schrijvers' outstretched leg late in the second leg in Amsterdam.

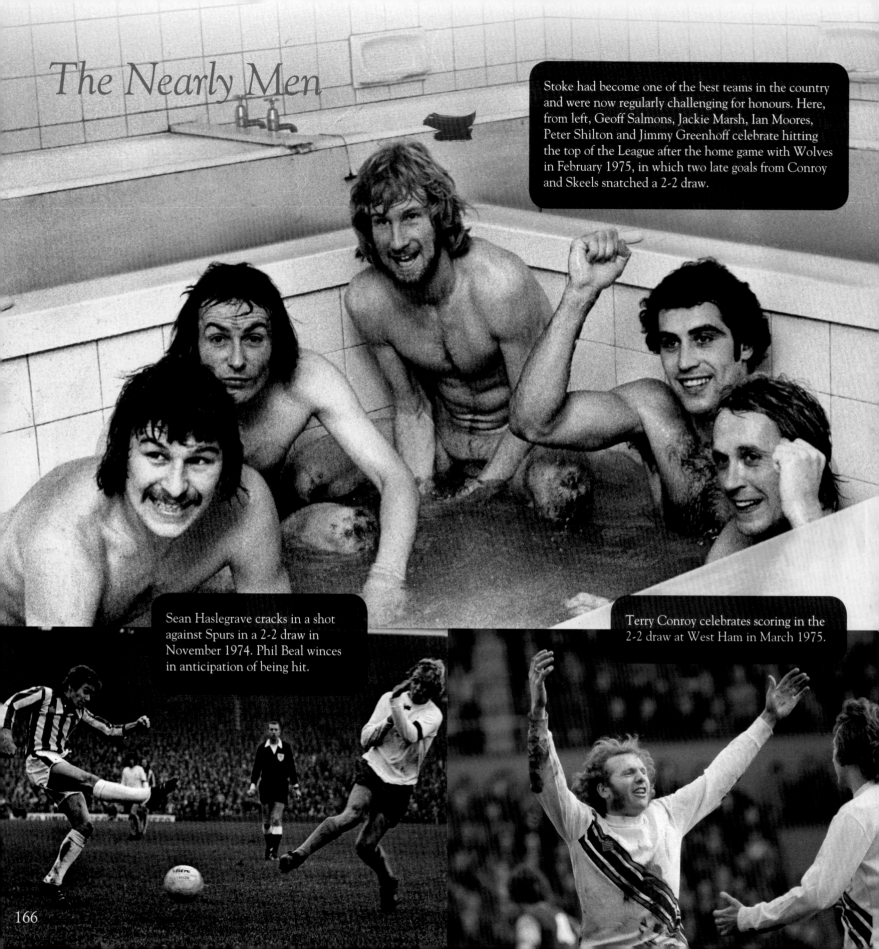

The Nearly Men

Stoke had become one of the best teams in the country and were now regularly challenging for honours. Here, from left, Geoff Salmons, Jackie Marsh, Ian Moores, Peter Shilton and Jimmy Greenhoff celebrate hitting the top of the League after the home game with Wolves in February 1975, in which two late goals from Conroy and Skeels snatched a 2-2 draw.

Sean Haslegrave cracks in a shot against Spurs in a 2-2 draw in November 1974. Phil Beal winces in anticipation of being hit.

Terry Conroy celebrates scoring in the 2-2 draw at West Ham in March 1975.

Stoke beat Liverpool 2-0 at Easter 1975 thanks to two classy Terry Conroy goals, and the
following week thrashed Chelsea 3-0 to top the table with just three games to go, although
they were level on points with Everton and Liverpool, with Derby just a point adrift with a
game in hand. Stoke would have won the title if they had won those last three matches, but
the four broken legs (Ritchie, Smith, Pejic and Robertson) which had accrued over the season
came home to roost, and a defeat and two draws saw the Potters finish fifth. Although City had
missed out on a first-ever championship, things weren't too bad as at least they had qualified
for Europe – or so everyone thought. UEFA decided to change the "one city one club" rule and
Stoke missed out as Everton took their place, having previously been denied it due to Liverpool
finishing above them. It would prove to be the first in a series of disastrous events which would
spiral out of control and cause Stoke City to become something of a laughing stock.

Jimmy Greenhoff comes close to scoring against Newcastle at the Victoria Ground in
April 1975. The game ended 0-0 and Stoke suddenly, after drawing two and losing one
of their final three games, found themselves fifth, not top.

Clowns to the Left of Me
1976-85

Stoke striker Lee Chapman takes on Manchester United's Arthur Albiston in January 1982 in front of a packed Boothen End and the new Butler Street Stand, built to replace its stricken predecessor, just in shot on the left

> "If you want entertainment go and watch a bunch of clowns."
>
> Stoke manager Alan Durban, 1980

1976 A storm blows the roof off the Butler Street Stand and Stoke have to sell several key players to fund its replacement. **1977** Amid a run of one win in 15 games, Tony Waddington leaves the club after 17 years as manager. George Eastham is appointed as manager but cannot save Stoke from relegation. **1978** Eastham is sacked as Stoke struggle in the Second Division. City humiliatingly lose at home to non-League Blyth Spartans in the FA Cup fourth round. Alan Durban is appointed as Stoke's third manager in a year. New signing Brendan O'Callaghan scores with his first touch just 10 seconds after coming on as a substitute against Hull. Paul Randall becomes Stoke's record signing, joining from Bristol Rovers for £150,000. **1979** Stoke win promotion in Durban's first full season in charge. **1980** Striker Garth Crooks is sold to Tottenham Hotspur for a record outgoing fee of £650,000. **1981** Lee Chapman becomes the first Stoke striker to score 16 goals in the top flight since Jimmy Greenhoff in 1973. Stoke avoid relegation thanks to a 3-0 victory over relegated Leeds United in the last game of the season. Durban resigns to become manager of Sunderland and his assistant Richie Barker takes over. **1982** Loyal servant Denis Smith plays the last of his 488 games for the club in 15 seasons' service. Barker signs Mickey Thomas, Sammy McIlroy and Mark Chamberlain, and Stoke play fabulous attacking football, almost winning a European spot. **1983** Barker decides to change tactics and employ POMO (Position Of Maximum Opportunity), resulting in numerous heavy defeats, several players leaving and his own sacking before Christmas. **1984** Bill Asprey becomes manager and re-signs Alan Hudson, and Stoke avoid relegation thanks to a 4-0 drubbing of Wolves on the final day of the season, with Paul Maguire scoring all four goals. **1985** Stoke set new records for the worst season ever in the First Division of English football, winning just three games, scoring only 24 goals and registering only 17 points.

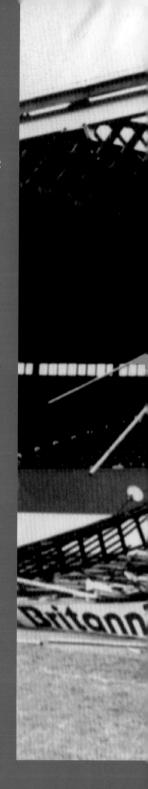

In January 1976 a freak storm blew much of the roof off the Butler Street Stand. It soon emerged that the stand was not insured and in order for its replacement to be built Stoke had to sell off their major assets – the club's best players. Alan Hudson joined Arsenal for £200,000, Mike Pejic went to Everton for £135,000, Peter Shilton signed for Nottingham Forest for £250,000 and, most controversially, Jimmy Greenhoff fetched just £120,000 from Manchester United. Greenhoff cried in Tony Waddington's arms in the Victoria Ground tunnel when he heard he was being sold. Supporters were devastated as the team was ripped apart.

In March 1977 Tony Waddington left the club, heartbroken at having seen his best players sold off. George Eastham succeeded him but could not stop the slide in results, which saw Stoke win just one of their last 15 League games. City suffered relegation on the final day of the season, despite only being in the bottom three for the last two games of 1976/77.

Waddington later managed former club Crewe from 1979 to 1981 and then retired from football, although he was made an associate director at Stoke in 1991. Arguably Stoke's greatest ever manager – it's a three-way discussion between Waddington, Bob McGrory and modern great Tony Pulis – Waddington died aged 69 in 1994.

Alan Durban

George Eastham's reign was neither happy, nor long. He departed in January 1978 after less than a year at the helm. While Stoke sought another manager the team was unceremoniously dumped out of the FA Cup by Blyth Spartans, with the non-League side winning 3-2 – at the Victoria Ground! This was arguably the single most embarrassing result in the club's history.

Hail to thee, Blyth Spartans!

By JOHN BEAN: Stoke 2 Blyth S. 3

TERRY JOHNSON scored twice as Blyth humbled Second Division Stoke. The Northern League side now travel to Wrexham to fight for a place in the last eight.

Blyth's pressure produced an inswinging corner from Bob Carney in the 11th minute that keeper Roger Jones fumbled and left top scorer Johnson an easy goal.

Blyth's brave challenge was checked inside three dramatic minutes of the second half.

In the 56th minute Viv Busby scored for Stoke when a Garth Crooks effort was luckily diverted into his path.

And three minutes later Crooks dived at the foot of the far post to head Stoke in front.

Equalised

But Blyth heroically pulled back to equalise in the 77th minute through Steve Carney

And two minutes from the end Johnson wrapped up the most memorable night in Blyth's Cup history by scoring the winner.

Alan Durban (nearest dugout, second from right) and assistant Richie Barker (on the left of Durban) watch from the Victoria Ground dugout. Note the fences around the paddocks, which were installed to keep home and visiting fans apart due to significant hooligan problems afflicting the game in the 1970s and 80s.

At one of the darkest moments of the club's history the Stoke Board turned to a young manager who had been having success with Shrewsbury Town, Alan Durban. Appointed on 13th February 1978, Durban moved to bring in several new signings who would become key players in the following season's promotion challenge. But no one could have foreseen how big an impact the first signing would have.

–LEGENDS–

Garth Crooks

Young black striker Garth Crooks was a quick, lively, sharpshooter with an accurate left foot, who dovetailed perfectly with "Big Bren" O'Callaghan. Crooks was born in Butler Street, at the end of which stood the Victoria Ground and rumours abounded of how he came to Tony Waddington's attention as a teenager after kicking a ball against the wall of the manager's office. They weren't strictly accurate, but no Stoke player could ever claim to have been quite as "local" as the boy born next to the ground. He would go on to find fame and fortune as a striker with Tottenham Hotspur, Manchester United, West Brom and Charlton, before sitting as PFA chairman from 1990 and joining the BBC – after retiring from the game that year – where he became renowned for asking long and convoluted questions in post-match interviews.

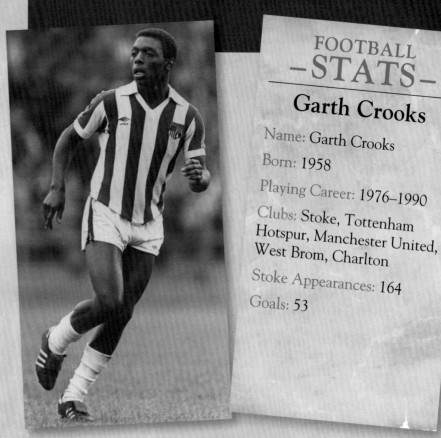

FOOTBALL –STATS–

Garth Crooks

Name: Garth Crooks

Born: 1958

Playing Career: 1976–1990

Clubs: Stoke, Tottenham Hotspur, Manchester United, West Brom, Charlton

Stoke Appearances: 164

Goals: 53

–LEGENDS–

Brendan O'Callaghan

No other player has made an impact in a Stoke shirt quite as quickly as Brendan O'Callaghan. Having just become new manager Alan Durban's first signing, from Doncaster Rovers for £40,000, and with the score against Hull City goalless with just 12 minutes left and the crowd clamouring for their new signing to be brought on as a sub, Durban turned to O'Callaghan and half-jokingly asked him to "Get me a goal." The instant reply came: "No problem." O'Callaghan jogged onto the pitch and rose to meet a corner at the near post to flick a header into the back of the Stoke End net with his first touch of the ball as a Stoke player. He had been on the field for just 10 seconds.

Stoke had lacked a big centre-forward since the demise of John Ritchie in 1974 and "Big Bren", as he became known, finished as leading scorer with 16 goals as Stoke won promotion in 1978/79. His heading ability was second to none, either attacking the ball to try and score or flicking on corners and free-kicks for others. His trademark thick walrus moustache and solid physique marked him out as a throwback to a bygone era and, in an age of fly-by-night stars, O'Callaghan also proved to be a great club servant.

He was versatile too. With Denis Smith injured, Durban converted O'Callaghan to play as an emergency centre-half in 1980. "Big Bren" took to the switch of role quickly and played comfortably there for several seasons.

Eventually, a groin injury hampered him and he was released by Stoke in 1985, joining Oldham, but his career was ended by the injury aged just 29 and he went on to have a successful career working for the Save the Children charity.

FOOTBALL –STATS–

Brendan O'Callaghan

Name: Brendan O'Callaghan

Born: 1955

Died: 2007

Playing Career: 1974–1986

Clubs: Doncaster, Stoke, Oldham

Stoke Appearances: 294

Goals: 47

Republic of Ireland Appearances: 7

Goals: 0

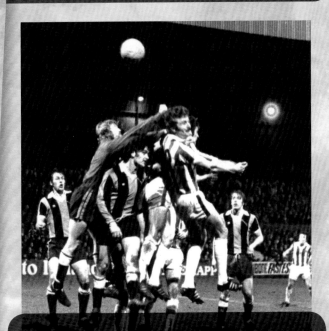

Brendan O'Callaghan scores within 10 seconds of coming on for his debut at home to Hull in March 1978.

Promotion Winners!

Powered by the Crooks and O'Callaghan forward line, ably assisted by new record signing Paul Randall, Stoke won promotion alongside Crystal Palace and Brighton back to the First Division, just two years after suffering relegation.

The 1978/79 promotion-winning squad: Back row (left to right, players only): Mike Doyle, Paul Randall (manager Alan Durban is third from left). Middle row: Adrian Heath, Alan Dodd, Roger Jones, Loek Ursem, Viv Busby, Paul Richardson. Front row: Sammy Irvine, Garth Crooks, Denis Smith, Brendan O'Callaghan, Geoff Scott.

Paul Randall, signed by Alan Durban from Bristol Rovers in 1978 for £150,000 – Stoke's new record transfer fee.

Midfielder Howard Kendall scores in Stoke's 4-1 victory over Charlton at the Valley in April 1979, a result which gave the team the impetus to go on and clinch promotion in the final game of the season.

Stoke lost just six games all season and the defence and goalkeeper Roger Jones set a club record of 31 for the fewest goals conceded in a season. A 4-1 win at Charlton at Easter prompted Stoke to push for a top-three finish. With four teams in contention; the ones to miss out eventually were Sunderland.

Great Game: 5th May 1979, Notts County 0-1 Stoke

Stoke won 1-0 at Notts County on the last day of the season thanks to this
86th-minute Paul Richardson header. The midfielder lunged to nod home
O'Callaghan's knockdown from five yards out to spark a huge crowd invasion
of Meadow Lane as hundreds of Stokies celebrated, knowing that victory
meant certain promotion. Stoke trainee Adrian Heath managed to get his
new leather jacket ripped amid the mayhem!

NOTTS
SOUVENIR PROGRAMME

WELL DONE CITY!
BEST OF LUCK FOR 1979/80

15p

v STOKE

–LEGENDS–

Peter Fox

The compact and agile Fox commanded his area well, believing that his defenders benefited from good communication from behind them, which would fill them with an air of confidence. Fox worked tirelessly for the club off the field and won the admiration of supporters. By 1981 Fox was being mooted in the national press as a possible England squad keeper, behind Ray Clemence and Peter Shilton. Ever present in 1980/81 and 1983/84, Fox fought off back injuries, and the challenges of deputies Eric McManus, Mark Harrison and Scott Barrett, to keep his place. Famous for his moustache and beaming smile, Fox was ever popular with the fans, being voted as Player of the Year in 1980/81, 1981/82 and 1989/90, a season in which he saved four consecutive penalties.

He starred as Stoke beat Stockport 1-0 in the Autoglass Trophy final at Wembley in May 1992; Fox's final appearance of the championship season in 1992/93, against Burnley, ensured he qualified for a championship medal – a fitting end to his career at the Victoria Ground, which saw Fox break the appearance record for a Stoke goalkeeper by a country mile.

Back in the Big Time

After achieving promotion in his first full season at the Victoria Ground, Alan Durban set about establishing Stoke in the top flight. He based his team on a solid defence, signing experienced full-backs Ray Evans from Tottenham and Peter Hampton from Leeds. Old warhorse Denis Smith was still going strong, although alongside him now was former Manchester City stopper Mike Doyle. The major change Durban made was between the posts as Roger Jones moved on to be replaced by young goalkeeper Peter Fox.

Peter Fox clings on safely once again – this time against Arsenal in January 1983.

Fox bravely dives in to stop Manchester United's Bryan Robson scoring in September 1983.

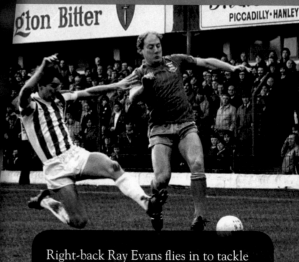

Right-back Ray Evans flies in to tackle Ipswich's Alan Brazil in January 1983.

In 1981 Ricoh became Stoke's first club shirt sponsors. Sponsorship was only just coming into the national game and many people objected to the fact that commercial slogans sullied famous shirts. It hasn't taken long for that attitude to have disappeared to be replaced with advertising on every conceivable part of players' kits! Here, club captain Denis Smith sports the first Ricoh shirt.

Denis Smith was constantly getting injured! Here he accepts a birthday cake in 1981 from the matchday mascot before the last match of the campaign (Stoke finished 11th) against Wolves. The following season Stoke became embroiled in a tense relegation battle and Smith starred in a 3-0 victory over Leeds United in the last home game of the season, which would prove to be his final game for the club and kept Stoke in the top flight for another year.

Send in the Clowns!

In 1979 Stoke produced a fantastic defensive performance to draw 0-0 at Highbury and take a point off Arsenal. The following season manager Alan Durban tried to do the same thing again, blocking Arsenal's path to goal with a team packed with defenders. It didn't work and Arsenal won 2-0, prompting questions in the post-match press conference about how "entertaining" Stoke's approach to the game was. Durban famously replied: "If you want entertainment go watch a bunch of clowns!"

The Stoke squad in 1981.

Lee Chapman celebrates scoring the only goal of the game at Highbury in August 1981.

The year after Durban's famous "clowns" comment, Stoke's match with Arsenal was interrupted with more frivolity as a dog stopped play by getting onto the pitch. Here Arsenal's goalkeeper Pat Jennings catches the interloper. Jennings would not be laughing by the end of the game, though, as

Alongside Chapman, Adrian Heath formed a young, tigerish strikeforce, but, at the end of the 1981/82 season, both were allowed to leave and manager Durban also moved on – to Sunderland. Heath would win League titles, FA and UEFA Cups with new club Everton, while Chapman would achieve similar feats with Leeds United, Sheffield Wednesday and Nottingham Forest, after an initial abortive spell at Arsenal, who paid Stoke £500,000 for his services.

–LEGENDS–

Lee Chapman

Following Garth Crooks' sale to Tottenham in the summer of 1980, Durban unearthed another gem of a striker – Lee Chapman. The burly centre-forward was blessed with film-star good looks, dashing haircut and the ability to be in the right place at the right time. He was capable of scoring spectacular goals, but also was happy to chest one in from two yards. Chapman's finest hour in a Stoke shirt came when he netted a hat-trick in a 3-1 victory at Leeds. He also scored the winning goal when Stoke went back to Highbury in August 1981 and won 1-0, thus cocking a snook at those "clown" headlines of the previous season.

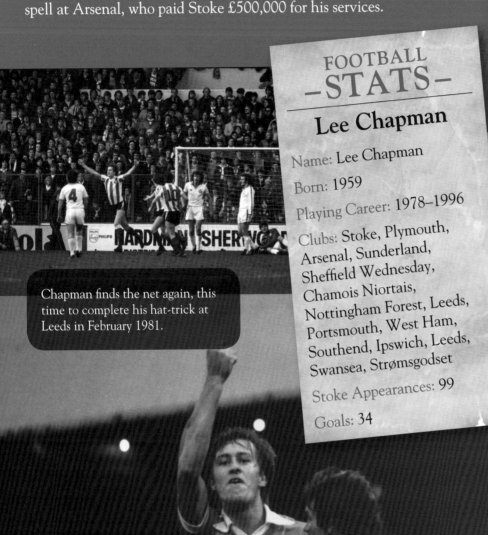

Chapman finds the net again, this time to complete his hat-trick at Leeds in February 1981.

Chapman celebrates scoring against Wolves in a 2-1 win at the Victoria Ground in April 1982. The big striker's relationship with the Boothen End was slightly hit and miss. But when he scored they loved him as one of their own.

Mickey Thomas – Chief Clown!

In the summer of 1981 Durban's assistant Richie Barker was promoted to the manager's hot seat. Barker initially endeavoured to push Stoke towards a more attacking style of football and he made three new midfield signings, which would change everything – Mickey Thomas, Mark Chamberlain and Sammy McIlroy.

Mickey Thomas is the butt of a training ground joke for once as Stoke's squad gain revenge for numerous pranks by debagging the Welsh midfielder.

Thomas was perpetually in trouble with referees, amongst many others!

Thomas celebrates in front of a jubilant Boothen Stand enclosure at the Victoria Ground after his 30-yard strike had earned Stoke a point in a 1-1 draw against Liverpool in October 1982.

–LEGENDS–

Mickey Thomas

The irrepressible Mickey Thomas holds a very special place in Stoke fans' hearts. He joined the club with something of a reputation following controversial spells at Manchester United, Everton and Brighton, after initially making his mark at home club Wrexham. Thomas' wife could not settle on the south coast and, after just one season at the Goldstone Ground, he sought a club closer to home and Barker risked £200,000 on Thomas in August 1982.

The impish Thomas was a bundle of energy that did not stop running on the pitch – or off it. "He was a scoundrel," Barker rather austerely recalled. "He was the best runner at the club and he could be up all night in London, sleep in the Chelsea bootroom, drive up to Stoke for quarter to ten and still lead the cross-country in training!" But Thomas took to life at Stoke – so much so that, by his own admission, he produced much of his best football at the Victoria Ground. His arrival completed the midfield of Chamberlain, Bracewell, McIlroy and Thomas – each one an international and all at, or around, their peak. Thomas revelled in the fluid play which propelled Stoke towards Europe, and finished the 1982/83 season as leading scorer with 13 goals. Stoke fans loved his cheeky style and revered his commitment – exemplified by his attempt to play on during the 4-4 draw with Luton when he badly gashed his leg. His obvious disappointment at having to be substituted endeared him to the Boothen End and, unsurprisingly, Thomas won the Player of the Season poll hands down.

Thomas joined Chelsea in January 1984 for a bargain £75,000, but it was not to be the end of the love affair between Stoke fans and this effervescent player. Alan Ball made arguably his shrewdest move as Stoke manager when he brought Thomas back to the Victoria Ground on loan at the end of the 1989/90 season as City hurtled towards the Third Division. Thomas jumped at the chance to sign permanently at the start of the following season, which rejuvenated his career at the age of 36. He won Player of the Year by a mile once again, despite obviously struggling with the demands of a full season of football, and at 36 years and 308 days played his final game for Stoke on the last day of the 1990/91 season.

FOOTBALL –STATS–

Mickey Thomas

Name: Mickey Thomas

Born: 1954

Playing Career: 1972–1993

Clubs: Wrexham, Manchester United, Everton, Brighton, Stoke, Chelsea, West Brom, Derby, Wichita Wings, Shrewsbury, Leeds, Stoke, Wrexham

Stoke Appearances: 57

Goals: 14

Wales Appearances: 51

Goals: 4

Chamberlain leaves two West Brom defenders (right) and several Spurs players (below) trailing in his wake as his one-man destruction of First Division defences continues.

Chamberlain's impact on the top flight was such that he won a monthly award for Player of September 1982, given by *Match* football magazine, and was selected by new England manager Bobby Robson to play international football, scoring on his debut.

Wing Wizard

Mark Chamberlain leaves West Ham's Alan Devonshire in a heap. Stoke won this game 5-2 in November 1982 in a fabulous display of attacking football.

Chamberlain hammers in a shot against Brighton in a 3-1 win over the south coast club in October 1982.

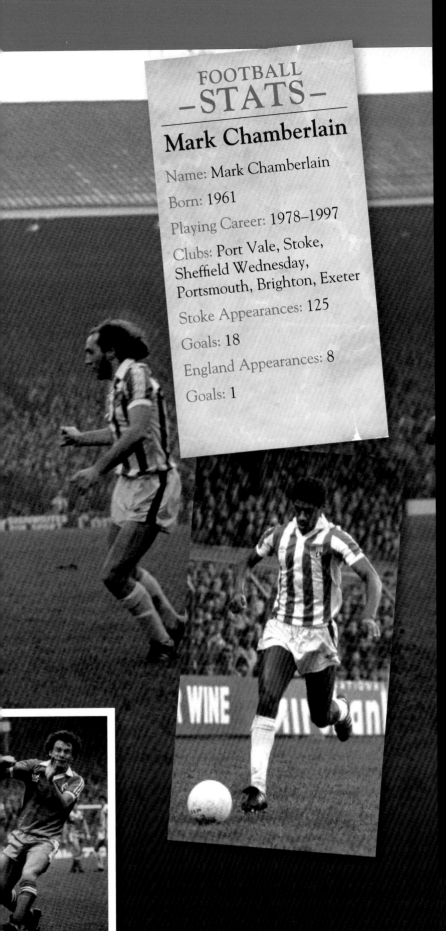

FOOTBALL
–STATS–

Mark Chamberlain

Name: Mark Chamberlain

Born: 1961

Playing Career: 1978–1997

Clubs: Port Vale, Stoke, Sheffield Wednesday, Portsmouth, Brighton, Exeter

Stoke Appearances: 125

Goals: 18

England Appearances: 8

Goals: 1

Mark Chamberlain

Arguably Richie Barker's greatest transfer coup was to swoop to make a double signing and bring goalkeeper Mark Harrison and winger Mark Chamberlain from Fourth Division City rivals Port Vale to Stoke for just £181,000.

Chamberlain became a firm favourite after he dazzled on his debut, running rings round England and Arsenal left-back Kenny Sansom as City won 2-1. He then notched his only hat-trick against Birmingham at St Andrews the following Saturday, as Stoke cut loose with a fabulous display of attacking football to win 4-1. He continued to take the First Division by storm and by November had won his first England cap, under new manager Bobby Robson, as a substitute against Luxembourg at Wembley. Chamberlain scored the quickest ever England debut goal just three minutes after coming on, with a flying header in a 9-0 win. For two years he was only rivalled as the country's best winger by Watford's John Barnes.

Chamberlain's slim, athletic build made him seem taller than his 5ft 9in height. His dribbling style was upright with chest puffed out, with the ball in front being almost toe-ended on by his right foot, while his arms worked like pistons. A favourite trick saw Chamberlain wave his left foot over the ball and wiggle his hips before jagging it past the defender with the outside of the right foot. A natural sprinter, Chamberlain was blessed with fast twitch muscles and he believed he could outpace every man he faced. Most times he was right. He starred in England's first ever win in Brazil in the summer of 1984, although his thunder was stolen by Barnes's wonder goal in the Maracanã.

His sensational form was sadly halted by a series of hamstring injuries, which reduced his speed. After Stoke's relegation in 1985, Chamberlain was sold to Sheffield Wednesday for a measly £300,000, settled at tribunal.

Sammy McIlroy

One of the best British midfielders of the late 1970s and early 1980s, Sammy McIlroy brought an experienced head to manage Stoke's numerous exciting youngsters from the centre of the field. Alongside emerging talent Paul Bracewell, McIlroy prompted Stoke forward as the side challenged for a European place in 1982/83. Famous as the last player to be signed by Sir Matt Busby for Manchester United, McIlroy made his first-team debut at 17 and played in United's winning FA Cup final team in 1977. He was on the losing side in 1976 and also scored in the 2-3 defeat by Arsenal in the 1979 final. In 10 seasons at Old Trafford McIlroy made 342 League appearances, scoring 57 goals. He scored on his Stoke debut in a 2-0 win at Sunderland in February 1982 and then starred as captain at that summer's World Cup finals for Northern Ireland as the underdogs almost reached the semi-finals, notably defeating hosts Spain 1-0 in Seville along the way. McIlroy was given a free transfer at the age of 31 after Stoke's relegation in 1985.

Arsenal's Alan Sunderland tackles Sammy McIlroy in full flight.

The police move in to break up a disturbance between West Ham and Stoke fans in November 1982.

A young fan clings to a fence in dismay as the discharge of a smoke bomb fills the away enclosure at Goodison Park. Stoke lost 0-1 to Everton in August 1983.

Hooligans!

Sadly, the 1970s and 80s were blighted by the spectre of hooliganism and Stoke were affected as much as any other club. Based in a working-class area, suffering from the high unemployment of Thatcherite politics, the club had plenty of disaffected youths happy to make trouble.

Stoke attack the Town End of the ground against Notts County in May 1982.

Great Game: 2nd March 1983
Stoke 1-0 Manchester United

Stoke had been striving to defeat Manchester United since returning to the top flight in 1979 and had come close on a couple of occasions, but finally, in March 1983, Brendan O'Callaghan's diving header from a Mark Chamberlain cross flew past United keeper Gary Bailey to secure an important victory for Stoke. It left them eighth in the division with only 14 games to go. Sadly Stoke couldn't keep up their impressive form and they finished 13th. Scant reward for such a wonderful 1982/83 season.

(Above) Brendan O'Callaghan stoops to head home Mark Chamberlain's cross to give Stoke a 1-0 victory over Manchester United in March 1983. (Below) "Big Bren" celebrates in front of the Boothen End.

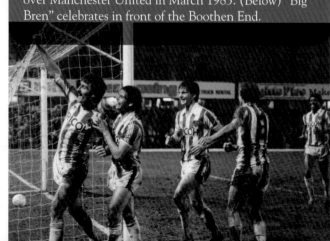

Ooh Georgie Berry!

ABOVE: George Berry has his famous afro combed.

-LEGENDS-

George Berry

The darling of the Boothen End for most of the otherwise-depressing 1980s, Berry was a central defender who made up for his lack of natural skill on the ball with his determination and commitment. A superb header of the ball, Berry became part of the near-post corner-kick routine with Paul Maguire and Brendan O'Callaghan, which caused havoc amongst opposing defences. Indeed Berry claimed that his bushy Afro haircut, on which he prided himself and which brought him so much stick was "the mother, father, son and daughter of all Afros" and was in fact a tactic. Its voluminous nature made it impossible for defenders to see past him until the ball was flicked on.

Berry lost the club captaincy under Bill Asprey and barely played, but after Stoke's horrendous relegation season of 1984/85, under new manager Mick Mills, Berry regained the armband on Alan Hudson's retirement. Now shorn of his trademark haircut, but sporting a thick beard, Berry formed a particularly strong central defensive partnership with Steve Bould, which helped Stoke to come within a whisker of the play-offs in 1986/87.

During this period, George's special relationship with Stoke fans deepened. Although wholehearted and committed, Berry was prone to occasional clanging mistakes (Peter Fox recalls "George used to think he was Beckenbauer!") and in March 1987 an overconfident pass across the back four instead found Brighton's Kevin Wilson, who scored after just 28 seconds, leaving promotion-chasing Stoke chasing the game against the bottom club. Berry was up for anything which involved fans and a bit of fun. In 1989 he competed in a "Milkathon" for the BBC Radio Stoke "Send a Cow to Uganda" appeal and milked Daisy dry of 2½ gallons to great acclaim! So established was George at Stoke that he was even given his own evening show on a local radio station, in which he played his favourite soul music.

Amazingly, manager Mills appointed Berry as penalty taker after both Graham Shaw and Keith Bertschin had missed from the spot. "Everybody fell about laughing when I handed George the job," recalls Mills, but Berry's confidence allowed him to be inordinately successful from the spot, missing only once, against Brighton in November 1989.

His eight years' service was rewarded with a testimonial game against Port Vale in August 1990, which Stoke won 1-0. Substituted on 30 minutes, Berry kissed the turf to rapturous applause, got changed and spent part of the second half standing with his beloved fans on the Boothen End.

Barker's Mad Tactics

Richie Barker (centre): The manager who built a fantastic and exciting team one season and then, in one fell tactical swoop, destroyed it.

BELOW: There were those that believed Stoke's new thin, pinstripe shirt was jinxed. It certainly was a huge departure from the traditional red-and-white stripes. It is sported here (from left) by Mark Chamberlain, Paul Maguire and Sammy McIlroy, who are all celebrating Maguire's successful penalty against Arsenal in the 2-0 win in Alan Hudson's comeback match in January 1984.

In the summer of 1983 Stoke manager Richie Barker attended several FA coaching courses and became a disciple of a system known as POMO – Position Of Maximum Opportunity. This essentially boiled down to defenders launching long balls to the edge of the opposition's penalty area where strikers would benefit from chances being created by pressure and mistakes. In reality it meant completely ignoring Stoke's greatest strength – the talented midfield and wide players at Barker's disposal. They soon became disaffected and both Bracewell and Thomas left quickly after the manager's conversion to the long-ball game. The tactic didn't work for Barker, either, and with Stoke having won just two games out of the first 19 and with only 12 points on the board, he was sacked on 9th December 1983.

Coming Back from the Dead

The return of Alan Hudson in January 1984, in particular, resurrected Mark Chamberlain as an attacking force as Hudson realized that the timing of his pass would release the winger whilst in full flight and leave the full-back on the half-turn, unbalanced and ripe for the picking. Stoke's scintillating form in the second half of the season saw them improbably battle clear of relegation. Sitting 21st with just 12 points before defeating Norwich on Boxing Day, Stoke won 10 of their last 18 games – including a wonderful display to defeat European Champions and League title-holders Liverpool 2-0 at the Victoria Ground on Easter Saturday – to survive.

ABOVE: January 1984: Alan Hudson returns to Stoke, and in his first match (right) City defeated Arsenal 1-0 to begin a complete turnaround in fortunes, when all had seemed lost.

On a dramatic final day of the 1983/84 season Stoke needed to win to stay up. Their opponents were the already-relegated Wolves, who had accumulated just 29 points all season and had conceded 80 goals. Stoke romped to a 4-0 victory to complete a remarkable survival bid. Equally remarkable, midfielder Paul Maguire scored all four goals, including two penalties (one seen here), and was then released on a free transfer that summer by manager Bill Asprey.

The Holocaust Season

Stoke may have survived by the skin of their teeth the previous season but they were everyone's favourites to be relegated in 1984/85, and the pundits and bookmakers were proved right. Stoke's season was an utter disaster. They set numerous unwanted club records including longest run without a win: 17 games (15th September 1984 to 22nd December 1984); fewest victories in a season: three wins; fewest goals scored in a season: 24 goals; and longest period without scoring a goal: eight League games (29th December 1984 to 16th March 1985)

Stoke put only 17 points on the board, a new record low for any club in the English First Division, which has only been beaten twice since, by Sunderland (15 in 2005/06) and Derby (11 in 2007/08). Manager Bill Asprey was sacked midway through the season after suffering from heart problems brought on by the stress. The season was completed by 10 successive League defeats. Stoke City were at one of the lowest ebbs of their history. Where could the club go from here?

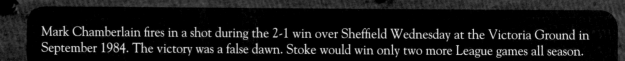

Mark Chamberlain fires in a shot during the 2-1 win over Sheffield Wednesday at the Victoria Ground in September 1984. The victory was a false dawn. Stoke would win only two more League games all season.

Tempers fray as Stoke lose 0-2 to eventual champions Everton in April 1985. The 1984/85 season was a horrible one for all Stoke supporters.

A true collector's item – one of Stoke's 24 goals in the 1984/85 season. Here striker Ian Painter cracks a penalty past Watford keeper Tony Coton in November 1984. It didn't matter as Watford won 3-1 at the Victoria Ground to leave Stoke adrift at the foot of the table. They didn't recover.

The Boothen Ends
1985-97

Forgive me Delilah, I just couldn't take any more!

Banner at the last game at the Victoria Ground, 1997

"

Stoke fans on the Boothen End bid farewell to their home of 119 years.

1985 Former Ipswich and England captain Mick Mills is appointed manager. Mark Chamberlain moves to Sheffield Wednesday for a paltry tribunal fee of £300,000. Stoke thrash Leeds United 6-2. **1986** Stoke thrash Leeds United 7-2. **1987** City's fantastic Christmas form of eight wins from 10 games pushes them into play-off contention, but they fall just short. **1988** Lee Dixon is sold to Arsenal for £300,000. Steve Bould is sold to Arsenal for £390,000. Mills spends over a million pounds on new players but the team does not gel. Stoke are thrashed 0-6 at West Brom, but would not lose another game against their local rivals for over a decade. **1989** Mick Mills is sacked after a 0-6 defeat at Swindon, with assistant manager Alan Ball taking over. **1990** Stoke are relegated to the Third Division for only the second time in their history. **1991** Ball departs acrimoniously after a 0-4 hammering at Wigan. Lou Macari is appointed as manager. Mark Stein is rescued from Oxford reserves and becomes a club legend scoring 68 goals in 123 games over just two years before being sold to Chelsea for £1.6 million. Stoke draw 2-2 at Anfield in a League Cup tie first leg. **1992** Stoke lose in the Third Division play-offs to Stockport County. City win the Autoglass Trophy at Wembley. **1993** The Potters win the Third Division title after setting a new club record for unbeaten matches of 25 and a new club points record of 93. Stoke beat Manchester United 2-1 in a League Cup first leg match at the Victoria Ground. **1994** Macari joins Celtic as manager and is replaced by Joe Jordan. **1996** Macari is back in the Stoke hotseat after he is sacked at Celtic and Jordan produces dull football at City. Striker Mike Sheron signs and sets a club record by scoring in seven consecutive matches. City lose out 0-1 on aggregate in the First Division play-offs to Leicester. **1997** Stoke say an emotional farewell to the Victoria Ground, their home for 119 years.

BELOW: Peter Fox (grounded), Steve Bould and George Berry (behind post) and Chris Maskery (arm raised) keep Sunderland's Eric Gates, Ian Wallace and Gary Bennett at bay in May 1986. Maskery, who made 92 appearances and scored three goals in six seasons at Stoke, later became known as the footballer fitted with a pacemaker after the midfielder's heart condition was revealed.

Stoke appointed former Ipswich and England captain Mick Mills as player-manager. In his first season in charge, 1985/86, the new manager found his feet and arrested Stoke's slump. But the following campaign saw his newly assembled team go goal crazy over Christmas as a great run of eight wins from 10 league games also saw the Potters smash in 29 goals to fly up the table into play-off contention.

Stoke's fantastic winter form included a remarkable 7-2 thrashing of Leeds, whose goalkeeper Mervyn Day crowed before the game that Stoke wouldn't put six goals past him again, as they had the previous season. Day was right, Stoke didn't score six, they bagged seven!

The campaign also saw City's best FA Cup run since the heady days of the semi-finals in the 1970s. After defeating Grimsby in a second replay 6-0 and Cardiff 2-1, Stoke were drawn against First Division Coventry at home. A tight match was settled by Micky Gynn's goal for the visitors. But there was controversy when Dave Phillips felled Stoke full-back Lee Dixon as he charged into the penalty area. Referee Nixon refused to give what was an obvious penalty, and, to rub in the misfortune, Coventry went on to win at Wembley! Stoke's FA Cup hoodoo had struck again.

ABOVE: Mick Mills proudly shows off the UEFA Cup which his Ipswich team had won in 1981. Stoke appointed Mills as player-manager in the summer of 1985 hoping his experience and winning mentality would steady a rapidly sinking ship.

LEFT: A magnificent seven goals flew past Leeds goalkeeper Mervyn Day at Christmas 1986.

Steve Bould and Lee Dixon had turned into highly regarded defenders under Mills' tutelage, and both were sold to Arsenal, having attracted Gunners boss George Graham's attention. Dixon fetched £300,000 in February 1988 and Bould £390,000 four months later. Both would go on to become bastions of the famous Arsenal back four which lifted countless silverware in the next 15 years.

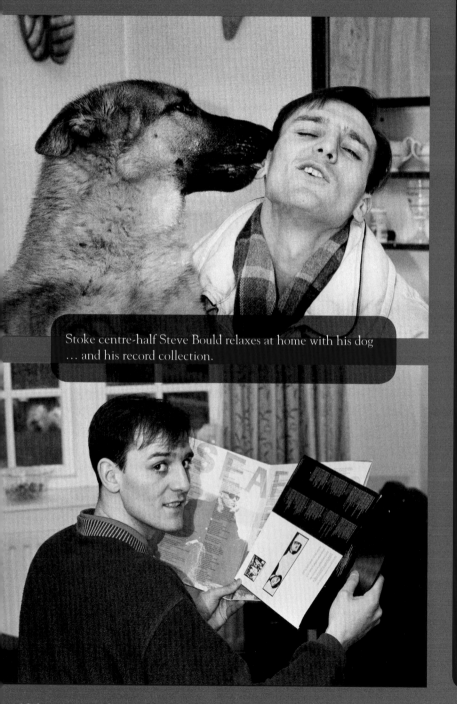

Stoke centre-half Steve Bould relaxes at home with his dog … and his record collection.

–LEGENDS–

Steve Bould

Despite standing 6ft 2in tall, Steve Bould began life in Stoke's first team as a full-back. The gangly Bould found it difficult to play on the flank due to his high centre of gravity and did not possess good enough passing ability to play one-twos to extricate himself from being caught with his back to the touchline. But after this tough introduction he grew in stature after Alan Hudson persuaded Bill Asprey to move him to centre-half. The young defender's performances earned the fans' respect to such an extent that they voted him Player of the Year for 1983/84.

After the debacle of 1984/85 Bould became the mainstay of Mick Mills' stabilization of the club. Mills offloaded the pedestrian Paul Dyson to West Bromich Albion for £60,000 and signed Lee Dixon from Bury for £50,000 in the summer of 1986. Bould developed into the best centre-half in the First Division and he attracted the attention of a number of managers, including Colin Harvey at Everton and Arsenal's George Graham, who were particularly impressed with Bould's ability on the ball. Late in the 1986/87 season, with Bould in prime form, a back injury, which required surgery, kept him out of the side from 14th March. Stoke's form slumped. The side had played its way into the play-off places, but without Bould the defence leaked 17 goals in 12 games, winning only four, to miss out on the chance of promotion.

Having also been watched closely for some time by George Graham, Lee Dixon joined Arsenal for £300,000 in February 1988. Bould followed that summer, and the pair shared in the glory of three League titles, three FA Cups, two doubles, a League Cup and the Cup Winners' Cup under Graham and then Arsene Wenger. Bould also won two England caps and finished his playing career at Sunderland before coaching Arsenal's juniors under Wenger.

Lee Dixon (second from right) watches as a Barnsley shot flashes past Peter Fox's right hand and the post in October 1987.

Striker Nicky Morgan celebrates one of Stoke's four goals in a 4-1 romp at Bradford in January 1988. Stoke became known as a goalscoring team under Mills, but continued to have to sell key and promising players such as Bould and Dixon to make ends meet.

Mills' Million

In the summer of 1989 the Stoke Board backed their manager's judgement and gave Mick Mills a million pounds with which to secure key signings to improve the team and have a real go at winning promotion back to the big time. Mills signed centre-half Ian Cranson from Sheffield Wednesday for a club record £450,000, striker Wayne "Bertie" Biggins and midfielder Ian Scott from Manchester City for a combined fee of £415,000 and Derek Statham for £100,000. But the gamble spectacularly backfired as Stoke failed to register a victory until their 12th game and eventually finished in last position. Mills paid for this by being sacked after a particularly humiliating 0-6 defeat at Swindon in November 1989. He was replaced by World Cup winner and former Blackpool and Portsmouth manager Alan Ball, who had been working as Mills' assistant for six months.

Ball couldn't arrest the slide and Stoke were relegated from the Second Division for the first time since 1926. Despite this, thousands of supporters turned out in fancy dress for City's final away game of the season, a 4-1 victory at Brighton. Most were convinced that Ball would get City back up straight away, but when early season form fell apart and the side struggled over the winter of 1991, Ball's trademark flat cap and squeaky voice became symbols of Stoke's slump. The fans rebelled and a disastrous 0-4 defeat at Wigan in February 1991 resulted in Ball's dismissal.

From left, Tony Henry, Chris Kamara and Cliff Carr try to keep control of Kerry Dixon during a 1-2 defeat at Chelsea in May 1989. Striker Dave Bamber looks on from the distance.

LEFT: One of the shining lights in an otherwise gloomy period of the late 1980s was winger Peter Beagrie. Mills signed the tricky entertainer from Sheffield United for £215,000 in the summer of 1988 and he lit up the Victoria Ground, with drag backs, Cruyff turns and several extremely special individual goals, notably against Bournemouth and Barnsley, which he would celebrate by turning a backflip! Here he takes on Oldham's Rick Holden. Beagrie was sold to Everton for £750,000 in October 1989.

RIGHT: Alan Ball celebrates the opening of his new pub, two months after leaving the Stoke hotseat following a 0-4 thrashing at Wigan. Ball left Stoke in the lowest league position in their history, 14th in the third tier of English football.

Skip to my Lou Macari

Desperate to bring some belief back into the club, chairman Peter Coates appointed former Birmingham manager Lou Macari as the new Stoke boss in the summer of 1991. Macari slowly began to weld a team from the players at his disposal, and made several astute and key signings: midfielders Steve Foley, from Swindon for £50,000, and Nigel Gleghorn, from his former club, Birmingham, for £100,000, central defender Vince Overson for £55,000 and, in late 1991, striker Mark Stein, who had been languishing in Oxford's reserves for £100,000.

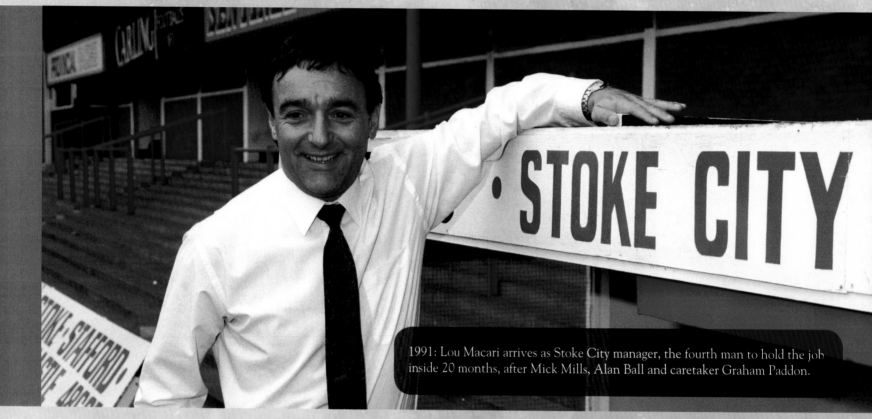

1991: Lou Macari arrives as Stoke City manager, the fourth man to hold the job inside 20 months, after Mick Mills, Alan Ball and caretaker Graham Paddon.

Great Game: Stoke 2-1 Manchester United, September 1993.

Stoke defeated Manchester United at the Vic in the League Cup second-round first-leg with Stein lashing both goals past Peter Schmeichel to the delight of a delirious home support. As he celebrated the goal by embracing the ecstatic crowd behind the Boothen End goal, Stein found himself booked by referee John Key, who, after the match, claimed he was acting on police advice!

But within weeks both Stein and Macari had both departed – the striker to Chelsea and the manager to boyhood club Celtic.

–LEGENDS–

Mark Stein

Hamstrung by lack of cash, new Stoke manager Lou Macari rescued Stein from Oxford's reserves in September 1991, initially on loan. Although he did not score in his first six games Stein's all-round play improved Stoke's form so much that Macari persuaded the Board to part with a paltry £100,000 in November and the goals soon began to flow. In February and March Stein rattled in 10 goals in 14 games as Stoke steamed to the head of Division Three. The League season ultimately ended in disappointment, although Stein gained revenge for Stoke's defeat in the play-offs by Stockport by ramming home a right-footed volley at Wembley to win the Autoglass Trophy final in May.

Standing just 5ft 6in and weighing just 11½st, the shaven headed Stein's speed off the mark and low centre of gravity rendered him a nightmare for opposing defenders. His scoring rate rocketed after the arrival of Nigel Gleghorn and Steve Foley, whose intelligent passes found him bursting through at pace to crack shots at goal first time. Stein tended to score well-struck shots rather than predatory goals inside the six-yard box – witness his stunning volley at Hartlepool in April 1992. City fans did not care how Stein scored, just that he did and reverentially began to refer to him as the "Golden One".

Stein's form soon brought interest from several Premier League clubs. In 1992 Kevin Keegan, the Newcastle manager, offered £300,000, but Stoke held firm, although Macari spent the summer of 1993 fighting off a bid of £1.2m from West Ham, while immediately prior to the start of the season, City rejected a £1m bid from Spurs. Stein eventually signed for Chelsea in October 1993 for £1.6 million, a club record outgoing transfer fee. In 1996/97 Stein returned to Stoke on loan for two months around Christmas and formed a promising partnership with Mike Sheron, scoring four goals in 11 League appearances.

(Left) Mark Stein nets one of his 68 goals in 123 games in just two years in his first spell at Stoke, this time against Burnley in a 1-1 draw in May 1993. Above, the "Golden One" collects his welter of Player of the Season awards after his 26 goals propelled City to the Second Division title in 1992/93.

The Autoglass Trophy

Captain Vince Overson ensures Stockport's Kevin Francis shall not pass during the Autoglass Trophy final.

Mark Stein lashes in the winning goal on a steaming hot day at Wembley…

… and celebrates in style!

The team enjoy that Wembley winning feeling as the supporters launch into a raucous rendition of 'Why, Why, Why, Delilah'.

In May 1992 Stoke were defeated in the Third Division play-offs by Stockport, but had the chance for revenge just three days later when they faced the same opponents in the Autoglass Trophy final. In a tight game, played on a baking hot day, Stoke's 34,500 fans drowned out Stockport's 10,000 or so supporters and delighted in Mark Stein's winning goal on 65 minutes. Captain Vince Overson lifted the trophy and the wild celebrations included a roof-raising verse of new club anthem, 'Delilah', which a Wembley spokesman later described as the loudest singing ever heard at Wembley.

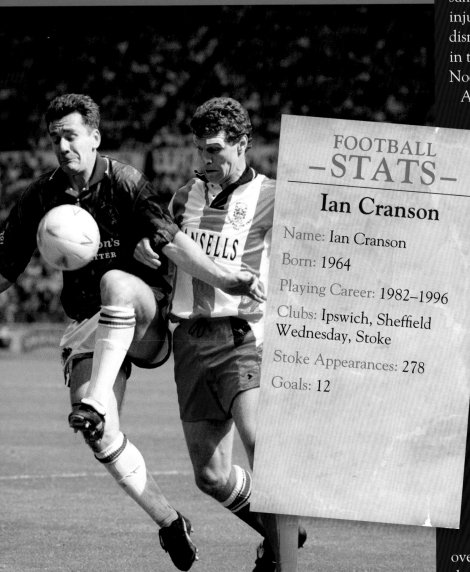

ABOVE: Ian Cranson helps Stoke keep a clean sheet in the Autoglass Trophy final at Wembley.

FOOTBALL -STATS-

Ian Cranson

Name: Ian Cranson

Born: 1964

Playing Career: 1982–1996

Clubs: Ipswich, Sheffield Wednesday, Stoke

Stoke Appearances: 278

Goals: 12

–LEGENDS–

Ian Cranson

A club record £450,000 was lavished on Sheffield Wednesday centre-half Ian Cranson by Mick Mills in the summer of 1989. Cranson was part of Mills' million pound spree that summer, but City struggled and Cranson suffered a nightmarish start to his Stoke career with injuries to both knees keeping him out of the bulk of that dismal relegation season, only making fleeting appearances in the Third Division as new manager Alan Ball preferred Noel Blake.

A solid, traditional stopper, Cranson's strength lay in his aerial ability. Wearing his trademark headband, he put the whole of his upper body and muscular neck into timing the ball perfectly from a characteristic two-footed leap. The arrival of Macari saw him become a regular starter and Cranson was an integral part of the team which won the Autoglass Trophy on an emotional day at Wembley in 1992 and the Second Division Championship the following season.

Cranson had a happy knack of scoring vital goals. In October 1991 he buried a header at the Kop end of Anfield as Stoke drew 2-2 with Liverpool in the Coca-Cola Cup second round first leg. A year later Cranson's late header from a corner gave Stoke a crucial 4-3 win against West Brom. He missed only one game in Stoke's promotion season and two in 1993/94 to earn recognition from City fans as Player of the Year as City re-established themselves as a First Division side.

Early in the 1996/97 season, Cranson was injured again at Barnsley, and this time Cranson could not recover fully. He retired on medical advice, totalling over 475 career appearances. He received a testimonial at the Victoria Ground in which Everton beat Stoke 2-0.

'Why, why, why Delilah!'

Stoke fans flood the Victoria Ground pitch to celebrate winning promotion thanks to a 1-0 victory over Plymouth in April 1993 with a heartfelt and vociferous 'Delilah'.

The Tom Jones song 'Delilah' had become associated with Stoke after an incident in a pub in Derby when the police asked a group of supporters, led by Anton 'TJ' Booth, to sing less rude songs. TJ opened up with his personal favourite – 'Delilah' – and the song stuck after being sung throughout the game that afternoon. The anthem soon became orchestrated into a choral extravaganza, led by TJ, atop a friend's shoulders, singing the lines of the verse, each followed by a chorused 'Oooooooh' from the massed Stoke fans, leading into the chorus.

ABOVE: The 1992/93 Second Division champions enjoy their moment of triumph at the end of a long hard season. Standing, from left: Graham Shaw, Paul Ware, Ian Cranson, Nigel Gleghorn, Peter Fox, Dave Regis, Carl Beeston. Kneeling in front: coach Chic Bates and manager Lou Macari.

LEFT: One of the stranger characters at Stoke during Lou Macari's reign was kitman Neil Baldwin, aka Nello the Clown. The former circus performer was a laugh a minute and even made it onto the pitch in one friendly against Aston Villa!

Anton 'TJ' Booth climbs up to lead another chorus of 'Delilah' on the Boothen End.

–LEGENDS–

Vince Overson

Shortly after his arrival at Stoke in 1991, Lou Macari signed one of his former players, the out-of-contract Overson from Birmingham for a transfer tribunal set fee of £55,000 – an absolute steal.

The barrel-chested leviathan had a physical style and voracious will to win that proved the vital ingredient missing from the Stoke team, Overson, at 6ft 2ins and 13½st, was a man-mountain. His colossal thighs thundered into challenges and his physical style of play, which often saw him give his opponent an early "reminder" of his presence, in the form of a rugged challenge, soon left Overson in trouble with referees.

Stoke's success of the next few seasons was built on the back four that Overson marshalled. After Overson lifted the Autoglass Trophy at Wembley he led the whole Stoke squad and the 35,000 fans at the tunnel end of Wembley in a rousing chorus of 'Delilah', which a Wembley spokesman confessed was the loudest racket he had ever heard at the "Venue of Legends".

Overson missed just four games at Stoke, with their best defensive record since the early 1970s, galloped to the Second Division title in 1992/93 and was voted into the PFA Divisional select XI by his peers. He left Stoke in 1996 after injuries curtailed his appearances.

ABOVE: Vince Overson proudly shows off the Second Division trophy, won under his captaincy in 1992/93.

FOOTBALL –STATS–

Vince Overson

Name: Vince Overson

Born: 1962

Playing Career: 1979–1998

Clubs: Burnley, Birmingham, Stoke, Burnley, Shrewsbury, Halifax

Stoke Appearances: 210

Goals: 7

Stoke won promotion back to the Second Division under Lou Macari. The team set new club records for longest unbeaten run – 25 games from 5th September 1992 to 20th February 1993 – and most points in a season – 93. Promotion was clinched with a 1-0 victory at the Victoria Ground over Plymouth on 28th April 1993. Gleghorn scored the winning goal after just four minutes, but victory was sealed thanks to veteran keeper Peter Fox's stupendous double save from Steve Castle.

Stoke established themselves in the First Division easily enough, but without talismanic striker Stein, sold to Chelsea, and manager Macari, who had moved to boyhood club Celtic. New manager Joe Jordan produced a functional but dull team, which was marooned in mid-table. With Jordan then sacked, in the summer of 1995 Macari returned as manager after a doomed spell at Celtic and City went close to winning promotion, losing 0-1 on aggregate to Leicester in the play-offs in 1996.

Farewell to the Victoria Ground: the End of an Era

After 119 years of football at the Victoria Ground, Stoke City decided that, rather than develop the old stadium in order to bring it into line with modern safety regulations and make it all-seater, they would build a new one. The final game at the Vic was against West Bromwich Albion on 4th May 1997. Prior to the match Stoke legends paraded in front of the Boothen End, then the largest remaining standing area at any English football ground. Above, from left: Johnny King, Terry Conroy, Don Ratcliffe and Sir Stanley Matthews take the applause.

Stoke fans bid a fond and tearful farewell to the Victoria Ground.

Two views of the Victoria Ground in the days before its demolition. Above, looking at the Boothen End and Boothen Stand from the corner of the Butler Street and Town End stands. Inset, the view through the Butler Street stand executive boxes.

High on the hill looking down across to the site of the Victoria Ground, the Britannia Stadium was being built ready to open in August 1997, opening a new chapter in this famous old club's history. The link between the glory days of the previous 119 years and this new home? A magnificent statue of the three ages of Stoke's greatest son – Stanley Matthews – which stands behind the new Boothen End.

The author would like to give a heartfelt thank you to:

All Stoke City fans for making our club so special. Particular thanks to Keith Wales, Martin Smith, Julian Boodell, Roger Martin, David Lee, Rob Stanway, Huston Spratt, Andy Peck, Monica Hartland, Norman Croucher, Steve Buxton, Nick Lucy, Manjit Sandhu and all the lads at the *Mirror* archive in Watford, especially David Scripps, the Sentinel, the Oatcake and Stoke City-mad. Apologies to anyone else I have forgotten to name, but you all know who you are.

Not forgetting Richard Havers for being a guiding hand and Paul Moreton of Bell Lomax Moreton for his tenacity.

Thanks to Nana for taking me down the Vic. Miss you every day.

But most of all to Mum, Dad, Jon, Kath and Evie. Love you all.